A Moved Soul

A Moved Soul

Boldly Responding to Encountering God

The Worth Pursuing Series: Part 1

Brenda A. Haire

A Worthy Press

Published by A Worthy Press
Chandler, Texas 75758
AWorthyPress.com

Library of Congress Cataloging: 2023937665
Paperback: 978-1-956673-81-4
Hardcover: 978-1-956673-09-8
E-book: 978-1-956673-10-4
Available in audiobook.

Scripture quotations are taken from the *Holy Bible*, New Living Translation, copyright ©1996, 2004, 2015 by Tyndale House Foundation. Used by permission of Tyndale House Publishers, Carol Stream, Illinois 60188. All rights reserved.

To protect the privacy of those who have shared their stories with the author, some details and names have been changed. Any Internet addresses (websites, blogs, etc.) printed in this book are offered as a resource. They are not intended in any way to be or imply an endorsement by A Worthy Press, nor does A Worthy Press vouch for the content of these sites for the life of this book. This publication is designed to provide accurate and authoritative information in regard to the subject matter covered. The advice and strategies contained herein may not be suitable for your situation. You should consult with a professional when appropriate. Neither the publisher nor the author shall be liable for any loss of profit or any other commercial damages, including but not limited to special, incidental, consequential, personal, or other damages.

Cover and Interior Design by TheJoyofPursuit.com
Cover Photo by Jamie Goode of JME Studios, Tyler, Texas
Hair and Makeup by The Meagan Brown

Prepare to Encounter God

As a thank you, enjoy a free guide to prepare for your next encounter.

BrendaHaire.com/Prepare

Other books by Brenda A. Haire

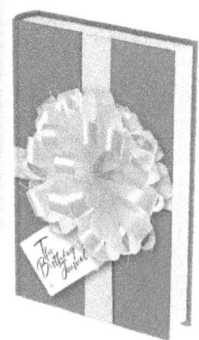

BrendaHaire.com/Books

To those wondering how all the pieces fit together.

CONTENTS

Foreword		XI
A Note from Brenda		XV
1.	Carpet Meeting	1
2.	Extraordinary	9
3.	Forbidden Scarves	13
4.	Dry Bones Rising	17
5.	Covenant People	25
6.	Preplanned	29
7.	Royalty	33
8.	Document	41
9.	A Moved Soul	45
10.	Colors Divine	53
11.	Progress Not Perfection	55
12.	Follow His Lead	81
13.	Avoid Heartbreak	87
14.	Torturing Yourself and Stifling the Spirit	91

15. God Is in the Details   95

16. Confirmation   99

17. Whoa, What a Night!   105

18. Spiritual Warfare   113

19. I See It   115

20. Stay in the Hold   119

Acknowledgments   124

About the Author   126

Start the Course   128

Hire Brenda to Speak   129

Stay Connected   130

Write Your Book   131

Buy in Bulk   132

The Worth Collection   133

FOREWORD

Whether you are a dancer or not, the encounter and response Brenda shares in the pages of this book will inspire you to move. You may not dance, but you will move! You will want to encounter God in a fresh way and boldly respond because you will see the transformation that is possible.

As a dancer for over sixty years and a prophetic dancer for twenty years, I'm thrilled when I hear others are called to the ministry of prophetic dance. There is a clear distinction between Kingdom dancing and prophetic dancing. Oftentimes, these are interchanged terms because there are two types of prophetic dance: choreographed and spontaneous. But just because a dance is choreographed doesn't mean it is *not* prophetic, and likewise, a spontaneous dance doesn't necessarily mean the dancer is dancing in the Spirit. Some dancers will feel called to dance ministry but not have the gift of prophecy through dance (and that's okay; there is a need for Kingdom dance). Prophetic dance isn't just steps; it's interpretive language through movement. It is prophesying with every movement. It is a powerful weapon in a spiritual battle most people aren't even aware they are in.

We are all in a spiritual battle. In fact, the enemy doesn't want you reading this book. He is probably telling you right now that you're not a dancer and that this book isn't for you. I'm here to tell you that this book is about *more* than dance. It's about encountering a life-changing God and what we do after the encounter. God, in His abundant grace, chose Brenda for this unique encounter because He knew she wouldn't keep it to herself. As she shares in her previous books, she has been called to write and knows this above all. She understands that God wants her to share her experiences and encounters to encourage and awaken others.

I'm tickled that God called Brenda to this at age forty-nine going on fifty. At sixty-eight years old, I continue to train dancers, travel, and teach on the subject, as well as usher in the Spirit through my gift of prophetic dance. God does not discriminate. Our age, or who the world deems capable of an activity, doesn't stop God from using those He has uniquely designed and gifted to dance prophetically. It's a unique calling for those mature in the Spirit, who understand the responsibility of revealing the glory of God through dance. Prophetic dance, as the name suggests, is a calling using the gifts of *dance* and *prophecy*. **If you are**

not called to this, then you're called to do something else. Your calling is as important as hers. Don't allow fear to hold you back from what God has and is calling you to do, no matter what it is. You are fearfully and wonderfully made. Let Him show you what He has in store for you and answer His call.

When Brenda first reached out to me, as she shares in Chapter 1, I had no idea what God was up to. Fast-forward to this book, and I'm in awe once again of our amazing God. Brenda has been glorifying God through her writing and speaking for years—faithful in the "little" things—and God knew she would surrender to this calling. I use the word *little* lightly, as there's nothing little about what she has allowed the Holy Spirit to do through her! But here's the thing about God: He knows our fullest potential, and He has plans that are bigger than anything we can conceive of or imagine. Whether you're encountering God for the first time through this book or He's using this to prepare you for what's to come, I know that you'll be changed by the journey Brenda shares.

Once again, Brenda is glorifying God through her gift of writing! Through this journal-style book, she is taking you in real time through what a calling looks and feels like, the resistance that rises up in all of us, and how His glory is revealed. We, the Church as a whole, need more believers like Brenda to take action when called! God has equipped you to do His work on earth. When we allow God to work through us, the heavens are opened! Regardless of your calling, because we love God, we are each uniquely called to do something magnificent for Him.

As you'll read, God uses the things we surrender to Him, and He is in the details of our lives. Brenda's joy in her writing is just as contagious as it is in person. Her accounts of this calling will prepare you to seek and respond to our Heavenly Father, who is waiting to bless you in ways you never thought possible. In this quick read, you'll understand that it's okay to question and why you should. You'll realize that you don't need all the answers upfront and how God unfolds the details as you respond. God will handle the outcome. We only need to handle our response. As Brenda encourages you to, be bold. Her faith is as contagious as her joy. You'll feel her fears, but she will show you her brilliance. This book is an example of blind faith. It's an example of what is possible. You'll see God in the details and learn how and when He speaks.

If you found this book because you are a dancer, you're in the right place. If you found it because you are seeking to encounter God, you're in the right place. If you are wondering how to respond to an encounter you've had, you're in the right place. As you can see, this book will expand your faith because it reveals the glory of God.

May His glory always be in motion.

—Janet Crews, Prophetic Dancer and Author of *His Glory in Motion*

A Note from Brenda

Hi! I'm bubbling with excitement to share this book with you. With a backlist of more than forty books to write, this one snuck up on me. It wasn't planned, but as you'll read, God has been working behind the scenes for a while now, and the timing is all His. I'm trusting Him and leaning in close as I move with Him.

This book was written in real time in response to an encounter with God, well into my walk with Him. That's the thing about encountering God—it's not a one-time experience. It's a relationship, and each time you encounter Him, it is fresh and new. Sometimes He teaches us from His Word and sometimes through His creations; at other times, He speaks to our heart, calls us to big adventures, or whispers quietly. No matter how or what He speaks to you during your encounters with Him, I hope this story will encourage you to take bold action in your response. And furthermore, I hope you write it down!

Write it down while the memory is fresh. There is a euphoria in new relationships that is often warned against. I recall before I met my husband, the singles' ministry I was part of encouraged me to make a list of the non-negotiables for a future spouse. Part of the reason for this was due to the euphoria we often feel when in a new relationship. When things are new and exciting, we can sometimes overlook red flags or flaws. It's not uncommon to forget about our core values because we are caught up in the moment.

This same euphoria can be experienced when encountering God, but the reason for writing down the encounter is profoundly different. When we experience a fresh encounter with God, our hearts may pound. We may feel invincible, and things that were once only dreams seem closer to reality than ever before. Our mind is filled with possibilities in those intimate moments.

Then we step back into our everyday life—picking up the children, taking the dog to the vet, commuting to the office, or making dinner—as routine and sometimes mundane as it can be. We discount the experience we had with God because we can't see how what He told us during our encounter fits into our "everyday life." We start to question if it was real. Did God really ask me to do that, say that, surrender that, or become that? *Surely not*, we convince ourselves, as we go about existing.

But here's the thing: God's Word doesn't promise us an existence. He promises us an abundant life.

The reason why most Christians aren't experiencing the abundant life is because they won't walk—*really* walk—with the One who promises it.

A bold response isn't sleepwalking. It is boldly and confidently stretching ourselves and relying on God to do what only He can do, while we do what He has equipped us for.

As I wrote in *Save the Butter Tubs!: Discover Your Worth in a Disposable World* and will likely write again, why do we trust God with our eternity but we can't seem to trust Him with our daily lives here on earth?

If God is calling you to something new, no matter how big or small, know that He is already there and has provided, or will provide, all that you need to succeed. Don't believe me? Try it for yourself. You'll stand in awe.

Not ready to test this yourself? Continue reading about how over the course of three months, God took my childhood dream of being a ballerina and breathed new life into it in a way I had never dreamed. If you would have asked me prior to October 10, 2022, anything about this, I wouldn't have laughed. Now I'm laughing with pure joy at what God can do if we allow Him to.

Enjoy the journey as I recap encountering God, responding boldly, questioning, battling, and receiving.

Chapter 1

CARPET MEETING
Monday, October 10-Day 107

I can't believe what God is telling me to do now. He is so fun, but He also makes me look crazy sometimes! I have learned, however, that I'd rather look crazy in obedience than become crazy in disobedience. If you're up for an adventure, keep reading.

At the turn of each decade in our lives, we tend to reflect or entertain expectations of what life will be like. I remember turning twenty with a sense of joy that I was no longer a teenager. For my thirtieth, my husband threw me a surprise party to ease the pain of crossing a more unsettling milestone. Forty came with another surprise party, and a sweet friend wrote a parody song about my next level. It was a fun party with photographs from my youth blown up to poster size and displayed all over the room.

Now, at the time of this writing, I'm one hundred and seven days away from leveling up to the big five-oh! A few months ago, I was with my youngest daughter, who says I'm still thirty-six in her mind, and I mentioned that I'd be fifty. The idea came to me to set a goal to achieve by my birthday. I want to accomplish something fabulous for my fiftieth. Not that I haven't had fabulous accomplishments up until now, but I want something to stretch me like never before. I've been kicking around some ideas, but nothing has grabbed my attention or my soul. Until today ...

As I'm typing this, I'm fighting back tears. You just never know what God is up to. I typically start my mornings in my prayer chair, aka massage chair. This morning, I was praying as I stepped out of the chair. I asked God what I should do first today. He said, "Carpet."

I hadn't been facedown on the carpet with God in a long time. I knew my body would hurt just getting on the floor and back up again, but I also knew I had to listen to Him. I questioned, *What could He possibly say to me with my face in the carpet that He couldn't say to me in my nice, cozy massage chair?* Well ... only God. He said, "You need to stretch." I questioned again: *Physically? Spiritually?* He apparently wasn't talking about my physical body just then. That came later. Let me back up and paint the picture.

Spiritual Health

After surrendering my life to the Lord, I've served in various ministry roles for decades. I released my first Christian nonfiction book, *Save the Butter Tubs!: Discover Your Worth in a Disposable World* in 2018, and the corresponding Bible study in 2021. By the time you're reading this, the guided journal to complement the series will be available with more books on the way. While I know that none of those things make me spiritually healthy, I share this to share about my obedience.

I understand my purpose in life is to worship God and bring Him glory in all that I do. Do I fall short? Yes! Do I tend to be a control freak and take matters into my own hands? Yes! This is why I believe He is stretching me. Stretching me *beyond* me. I can only accomplish what He is asking me to do through His Spirit. Literally! I'll explain more in a bit. For now, know that I know what it means to be facedown in the carpet with God, and I was surprised by His request and what He was speaking to me.

Physical Health

Darren (my "hubs/honey," as I like to call him) and I walk two to four miles almost every evening. We've been doing this for about fifteen years now. We also take hiking trips two to three times per year and hike an average of fifteen to twenty-five miles on each trip. In the past, I've completed four half-marathons and a sprint triathlon. But all the while, I have watched my weight yo-yo. And while I enjoy the benefits of weight training, it bores me.

Lately, I've been doing what I call microwave exercises—calf raises, push-ups, leg lifts, triceps extensions, et cetera—all while waiting for something like the microwave to ding or the shower to get warm or while brushing my teeth. I know, I'm strange. For someone who sits all day writing and working on a computer, any time I can physically move my body, I do. But I still wasn't seeing the results I desired.

Then in June 2021, I had a cancer scare that shook me. I knew everything had to change. I finally caved and allowed my doctor to prescribe a shot to help my body properly regulate insulin. I was headed for a full hysterectomy at the age of forty-eight and knew that with menopause comes weight gain. At 216 pounds, I couldn't afford to pack on more weight. I had to do something, and what I was doing wasn't enough.

I was hesitant about the shot because I don't like pharmaceuticals and didn't fancy the idea of giving myself an injection once a week. But after one month, I was down five and a half pounds, then six and a half, then eight and a half. Month after month, the weight kept falling off. Over a year later, it has plateaued, but I'm lighter than I've been in twenty-two years. I feel like I'm living in a new body. The strange thing is that I feel like I'm healthier in so many ways, and yet, my body is still hurting and reminding me that it's about to turn fifty.

Or is that just my limiting belief that turning fifty hurts physically? I'm not new to the world of fitness, and I know what to do; I just don't find pleasure in working out. I'd rather hike. I'd rather dance. Yes, *dance*. I love to dance. I love all types of dances. Unfortunately, my knees don't like it as much as I do.

I took ballet and jazz in middle school, danced country-western style all through my high-school years, and taught ballroom at Arthur Murray Dance Studio before joining the Air Force when I was twenty. I have always loved dancing. Just seeing a tutu gets my heart pounding. I love the form and beauty of ballet. I've taken ballet classes as an adult, but at the time, I couldn't see how it served me. Plus, I was carrying the extra weight and wasn't feeling in my element. I was, however, feeling the pain in my knees with every plié.

Then this morning, I'm on the floor with God. I hear Him say that I need to stretch, and I'm like, "Um, okay." I knew He meant spiritually, but as I began to sit up, I started to stretch and realized how tight all my muscles and joints were. Everything hurt. I took some time and stretched my muscles. Releasing the tension hurt but also felt satisfying. After I scraped myself up off the floor, I made a protein shake and headed to the dining room table for my Bible study time, thinking to myself, *I need to create a routine for this. My body needs this.* I've always known how good stretching and flexibility are for a body, but I neglected them nonetheless.

As any good Christian woman does, while enjoying my breakfast, I grabbed my phone and checked social media. (Kidding!) While scrolling, I came across a post my cousin Janet shared. It was a video featuring a beautiful prophetic dancer named Kimberly Brown-Phillips. I watched intently and was overcome with chills and tears. The Holy Spirit stirred as the song "Something Has to Break," by Kierra Sheard, was so eloquently brought to life by Kimberly's dance. After watching, I commented, "Chills and tears! So beautiful! Makes me want to take up prophetic dance."

I then moved to my Bible study time just moments later, after finishing my shake. Reading in Galatians while preparing for another book I'm working on, I was overcome with tears and felt God saying that this was my big "Fabulous at Fifty" challenge! *This is what God has for me this season?* I'm still in shock as I type this.

He is calling me to prophetic dance.

Full-Circle Moment

Just yesterday, I posted on social media, asking, "If you were to go as me to a costume party, what items would you need to complete the look?" Most answers included something about books and the color yellow, which totally aligns with me. But my good friend Tina said, "Ballerina costume." I commented back, "That was fun and will likely show up again!" And then today ... *Dancing? Really, God?*

Oh, my heart is so full right now. When I first started my speaking and writing ministry, I was praying one day about what I'd wear on stage. I wanted a signature look. I wanted to be comfortable but stand out in a good way—to be distinctive so that the message would be that much more memorable. (You see, I want to transform lives.) God spoke then too: "A tutu," He replied. I was like, "Um, I'm sorry, what did you say?" He repeated Himself, as He so graciously does.

So that year, I spoke to Tina's fourth-grade students as a ballerina. I spoke on the topic of purpose, giftedness, and outside-the-box careers. I remember one of the other teachers commenting that she wished she had heard my presentation as a child.

I haven't forgotten that comment over the years and have often wondered if that was for a season or something God wanted me to use going forward. Sometimes it feels like I've gotten lost in the weeds while finding my way as an author. If you read my first book, you know a bit about my struggle as a writer. That struggle carried over to speaking and the calling on my life to serve from the place I was first broken. What did God really want me to share? How would I glorify Him?

Today, I feel this is the full-circle moment. Before I opened my laptop to begin documenting this journey, I looked through my "Life Song" playlist and danced to two songs. It wasn't perfect—my endurance needs strengthening—but it was beautiful. I could feel the Spirit in a new way. Did my body hurt? Oh, yes! Did I care? Not one bit. I know that with time and His power, I'll be able to bring to the stage a beautiful prophetic dance. I've known for years that I've had the gift of prophecy, but never in a million years did I see this coming.

My goal is to surprise my friends and family at my fiftieth birthday party with a Spirit-filled prophetic dance. After this revelation started becoming clear, and before I could talk myself and—attempt to talk—God out of it, I reached out to my cousin Janet who shared the post. She's been a prophetic dancer for decades and recently released a book on prophetic dance ministry. I texted her before fear could set in—before I could excuse away this crazy calling.

Now, let the leaning in begin. I'm leaning into God and what He wants to come of this. I see things; I've seen them in my mind for years but never thought this would come to pass. I'm a busy business owner, author, speaker, and coach. I don't have time for a whole new thing. But God ... He is reassuring my soul that this isn't new. It's been buried. The dream to dance has been there since I was a child, lemon-skipping and interpreting songs in my driveway while my tape recorder blared atop my mother's car.

Chapter 2

Extraordinary
Tuesday, October 11–Day 106

T he author in me is struggling today with how to shape this memoir. I want to capture what God is saying and showing me in hopes that you will see how He works in the average, ordinary days—

Wait, what? Our days aren't average or ordinary when we are walking with God! The closer we draw near to Him, the more we are able to see the extraordinary that He creates and provides.

Today, I listened to my cousin Janet's recorded teaching that she sent me yesterday after my text. She held a master class recently, sharing about prophetic dance. It was very eye-opening. I'm going to be real and tell you that I have a lump in my throat and tears in my eyes. I don't know what God wants me to do with this calling to dance prophetically. I strongly feel this is a fresh call. He may have planted seeds long ago with the ballerina outfit. And by the way, I did wear it, and of all days to have a fire drill ... Yes, I'm afraid I was on the playground with the entire school while wearing a pink tutu! I look back now and think, *What was He doing then that I couldn't see?*

Fast-forward several years to when a friend invited me to attend the symphony with her. She had season tickets, and her husband was traveling. I jumped at the chance. There was a time in my life when I attended many shows, symphonies, and other performances. I hadn't realized until her invitation how much I missed those times. The experience was beautiful. My friend mentioned ahead of time that these were special nights for her and that she dressed up for the occasion. I love dressing up and agreed that I felt the same and would dress for the occasion too.

That night as the orchestra played, I choreographed an entire ballet in my head. It was magnificent. Afterward, we discussed the evening, and I shared my experience with her. She was stunned and asked if I considered myself a choreographer or dancer. I described my dance experience and told her I wasn't sure why, but that's how my mind hears and interprets the music. Today, Janet confirmed this gift in me when she explained prophetic dance. She said that if you see the music and can interpret what God is speaking to us through it, you are anointed in this area. I receive that.

I've known for years that I have the gift of prophecy. My former women's minister ushered in this revelation during a teaching on spiritual gifts. I was shocked because I didn't understand the meaning of the gift at the time. Having the gift of prophecy means to speak God's truth, to encourage, to exhort, to comfort, and to show others what God wants them to see.

This was part of the teaching I shared in my tutu to the fourth-graders. God wanted me to show them how they are each uniquely designed and that they could live on purpose and enjoy the journey. I instructed them to write down six things they are good at or really enjoy in one column and, in a second column, six jobs they are interested in. We made a game out of this and numbered the lists. Then we rolled big fuzzy dice and matched the activities/jobs that coordinated with the dice—one from each column. Here are my lists, for example:

1. Dancing	1. Author
2. Writing	2. Speaker
3. Seeing and sharing truth	3. Event planner
4. Problem-solving	4. Innkeeper
5. Dressing up	5. Retreat center owner/operator
6. Coaching	6. Teacher

If we rolled a two and a six, you'd get my current job. I teach book writing through my Author Business Network. If we rolled a one and a six, I could be a dance teacher. Or if it were a one and a three, that could be a recital planner, gala planner, and so on. To double the results, you could swap columns, so the two and six now become speaker coaching (what I do); one and six become author coaching (also what I do); and one and three would be an author sharing new insight (again, what I do).

It's a fun exercise I now call the "Fuzzy Dice Formula" and teach in my course, The Pursuit Process, to help people brainstorm and think creatively about what God has equipped them to do. Take a moment to try it. I'd love to hear your creative results and if any spark a new path for you.

I'm thankful for the gift of writing. Had I not immediately documented all that transpired yesterday with God, I wouldn't even believe it myself today. It seems like a distant dream. I'm even more thankful that by capturing it, I can share it with you to hopefully expand your faith in what God can do.

Yesterday, I shared a full-circle moment about speaking to Tina's fourth-graders. Here's another full-circle moment for me. In prophetic dance, often banners, flags, ribbons, and such are used to enhance the visual representation with color and additional movement. Are you ready for this? I was actually on the flag team in high school. Yep. We couldn't afford the cost of the dance team, and I hadn't taken enough dance to feel like I could qualify for the team even if money hadn't been an issue. I'm sure my mom would have found a way if I had been adamant about joining, but looking back now, I think God had other plans for that time in my life. He would use it to prepare me for this new calling. He wastes nothing. Funny thing, Tina was a big reason why I joined the flag team. We stayed with the team for two years, and then Tina stayed for her senior year as well.

I only have a glimpse of what God is calling me to do here, but I'm excited to see what He's up to.

Chapter 3

FORBIDDEN SCARVES
Wednesday, October 12—Day 105

Yesterday, I felt inspired to get up and dance after watching Janet's master class replay and writing. Since I don't currently have flags, ribbons, or banners, I improvised with some colorful vintage scarves. If you read *Save the Butter Tubs!*, you might recall the "forbidden scarves." I had so much fun dancing with two of them yesterday that I danced again this morning with two more.

Janet explained briefly in her master class about using colors to reflect the tone of the song. The scarves are solid, vivid colors—red, green, yellow, et cetera—about ten in all. Yesterday, I just moved my body however it felt right with the music. Today, I worked on choreography, replicating the movements for repeated phrases in the songs. It was a blast. I have no idea how good I am at this, but I know that it feels incredible. I even dug out my ballet shoes to protect my feet. I've experienced some pain, but I haven't been to the doctor for it just yet. It comes and goes, and this morning, I prayed God would supernaturally heal my foot so I could worship in this way. I felt absolutely no pain while dancing. God is so good. I was also able to walk a mile this evening with hubs, and it didn't bother me then either. Yeah, God!

Still not sure how any of this will play out. I'm focusing on basic ballet exercises to tone, stretching, and of course, prophetically moving to the music. I'm not sure yet what song I'll debut to at my birthday party, but I know I want to create an encounter with His glory for those in attendance.

I've also had some fun researching outfits and flags. I can't wait until Janet's manual, *His Glory in Motion: A Guide to Success for Ministry Dance Teams*, arrives. Not that I plan to build a team, but if God directs, who am I to say no? I also ordered Kimberly Brown-Phillips's book, *Utterances Unspoken: A Guide into Prophetic Dance Ministry*. I'm excited to read both. I'll likely order flags after I choose the song so that I can coordinate the colors to reflect its mood.

I'm not sure about the outfit yet. I know that it will be unlike any previous dance attire, as prophetic dance is more conservative than contemporary ballet. Many dancers wear long sleeves. I can't see myself doing that, but who knows? I've thought about a full-length tutu since I'm in love with tutus. We shall see. I'll remain in prayer about the attire as well as the song while I continue to train.

Since Monday, I've been amazed at my energy level and the amount of focus I have. I've also been extremely productive in my work. Not sure if this is due to the new release of obedience, walking closer to

God the past three days in a new way, or if it's my body thanking me for moving physically in a new way. Whatever the reason, I'm enjoying it all. I'd even say that I'm encountering His glory!

I still haven't mentioned this to anyone other than Janet. I'll likely share it with my dear friend, fellow author, and prayer warrior Andrea Fehr. As Janet mentioned in her training, intercession is vital in prophetic dance, as the spirit of criticism runs rampant. I'll certainly be praying more specifically from now until January. However, for those who live close enough to attend my birthday celebration and for my immediate family, I'd like to surprise them with this new experience, and I strongly feel that God wants me to keep this between Him and me for now. It's not about the approval or acceptance of anyone else.

A week ago today, I had the opportunity to attend my friend's son's baptism. Izek has a special place in my heart. I'm so thankful I was able to attend, and the timing of my seeing the post about it on social media, my availability, and specifics of the event ... well, God is up to something.

The evening was called "Encounter." I'm not sure how often this church holds this event or if the programming is the same each time, but this evening was all about encountering the presence of God. We worshipped in song, prayed, and shared the Lord's Supper. It was a beautiful evening, and the presence of God was tangible. The room was packed with all ages of people, singing and worshipping in their own unique ways. While no one was prophetically dancing full out, there were people gesturing with their hands. I usually worship with my eyes closed, but since they included a few unfamiliar songs, I needed to see the words on the screen, which allowed me to catch a glimpse of others worshipping. Coincidence? I don't think so. God orchestrated that night and everything else over the past week.

He's known my desire to celebrate my birthday with something BIG and outside of the norm for a while now. Honestly, I'm thankful it is something conservative and not a figure competition! That was once a thought I had. I just couldn't reconcile the idea of that tiny bikini and my ministry. The muscles and body shape—I'll take those, but I don't plan to do any rigid weightlifting. Unless God has other plans, I'll build my temple by worshipping Him through dance.

Chapter 4

DRY BONES RISING
Friday, October 14–Day 103

I missed writing yesterday. Didn't dance either and felt it in my spirit. However, I received both books, Kimberly's and Janet's. To make the most of my time, I took them with me to an event and read during my downtime. Once again, tears streamed down my cheeks as I encountered God in the pages. Janet wrote about choosing the right music and then quoted Ezekiel 37:1–10:

> The Lord took hold of me, and I was carried away by the Spirit of the Lord to a valley filled with bones. He led me all around among the bones that covered the valley floor. They were scattered everywhere across the ground and were completely dried out. Then he asked me, "Son of man, can these bones become living people again?"
>
> "O Sovereign Lord," I replied, "you alone know the answer to that."

Then he said to me, "Speak a prophetic message to these bones and say, 'Dry bones, listen to the word of the Lord! This is what the Sovereign Lord says: Look! I am going to put breath into you and make you live again! I will put flesh and muscles on you and cover you with skin. I will put breath into you, and you will come to life. Then you will know that I am the Lord.'"

So I spoke this message, just as he told me. Suddenly as I spoke, there was a rattling noise all across the valley. The bones of each body came together and attached themselves as complete skeletons. Then as I watched, muscles and flesh formed over the bones. Then skin formed to cover their bodies, but they still had no breath in them.

Then he said to me, "Speak a prophetic message to the winds, son of man. Speak a prophetic message and say, 'This is what the Sovereign Lord says: Come, O breath, from the four winds! Breathe into these dead bodies so they may live again.'"

So I spoke the message as he commanded me, and breath came into their bodies. They all came to life and stood up on their feet—a great army.

I don't recall the moment when God first gave me this passage as the ultimate calling on my life, but I believe God wants to awaken the church to be *the Church*. Let me explain. I was raised in a Catholic church until my parents divorced when I was nine years old. I didn't regularly attend church again until, as an adult, I came to know Jesus in an interdenominational church. I fell in love with Jesus and want nothing more than to be obedient to what God designed me to do for His Kingdom's sake. I have been active in some sort of ministry ever since.

Sadly, I've seen people from all walks of life who claim to be Christians but who are spiritually dead. The fruit is unseen. They check a box of going to church to feel good about their "ticket to heaven," but they aren't actually in a relationship with Jesus. Some Christians I've met are amazingly good people and show God's love to others but are still spiritually stuck. They judge the way others worship and live under man-made religion. They are not fully free in Christ.

I understand my gift of prophecy is to show them what true freedom looks like. The capital-"C" Church is the body of believers as a whole, and the small-"c" churches are not representing the body well. I believe it is time to rise and represent our God who is fully alive!

The very power that raised Jesus from the dead lives in us. Why does it seem then that most people are suffering from a power outage? It's because of their immaturity in faith. It's almost like an out-of-sight, out-of-mind experience. People believe in Jesus at the moment of salvation but don't believe in Him for anything else in their lives. They don't want to think about their own death, so they often don't recall the powerful moment when Jesus introduced Himself to them personally.

I never want to forget encountering His glory for the first time, for the many times since, or four days ago, facedown in the carpet, and all the ways since then He has confirmed this new calling. This is one of the reasons I'm documenting this process.

God has not changed the call on my life to raise dry bones. He is simply expanding it. Stretching me! God calls us to Him: first to follow Him, and then more specific calls to us based on our unique gifts.

I acknowledge the call from God to write and to heal the broken-hearted through sharing my story of brokenness. I felt that call so strongly in my spirit, and He continues to confirm it again and again. I share a bit of that journey in *Save the Butter Tubs!*. The ways God has healed me will show up in the more than forty books He has on my to-be-written list. Of this, I am certain: writing is a calling on my life.

Then He gifted me the opportunity to help others "awaken" and share their stories by providing me the wisdom and knowledge of all things publishing and building an author business. As I work with authors and witness the aha moments as I coach them toward their goals, I'm reminded of how significant this part of my calling is to furthering the Kingdom.

Now He is stretching me again with a new layer. The call is the same—awaken dry bones. He is using me in the unique ways He has made me to answer the call. All of this is so that *His* people may encounter *His* glory. So today, I danced.

Right now, I'm dancing to some of my favorite songs and awakening my body to the movement of dance again. It has been years since I danced like this. It's funny what God will remind us of as we walk in obedience. I've only had two recurring dreams my whole life. One was a childhood nightmare that I'm thankful I no longer dream. The second is of me dancing. Leaping really. I don't recall having the ability to ever leap the way I do in my recurring dream, but I'm going to start training for it. I don't believe God would give me that dream and then remind me of it now without reason.

My internet search history this week sure has changed, as I research proper techniques for leap training. I've also researched books, attire, flags, and more! God is already showing me visions for the cover of this book as well. I'm not sure I'm ready to be on a book cover, but that is what He is showing me, so I researched some dance poses. I've always had an image of a ballerina bowing in my mind. When I think of ballerinas, that is the pose I see. I'm imagining myself in a long tutu or tulle skirt. I'm thinking of a gold sparkly one. Maybe with a teal background. Or the opposite—a yellow background and a teal tutu. Who knows what will happen? Only God at this point. I have time to research and plan as I continue to dance and learn. I'm excited about it all and to see what He plans to do with this long term.

I did finally tell someone. I told Andrea in a video-chat program we use. I haven't heard back from her yet, but I look forward to it. She is someone I completely trust and who I know will lift me in prayer. I need that covering—the covering of the Holy Spirit. This is all so foreign but so personal at the same time.

When I think of my love for dance, I recall as a child standing on top of my grandpa's boots as he danced. This is how I learned the Texas two-step and the waltz. Then as I grew, my dad taught me more of a Western swing. I still love them all. Waltzing, when done right, is a beautiful dance I could do for hours. Spinning around the dance floor in a waltz feels divine to me.

I taught my children to dance and love dancing with my daughter Beth. She's a fantastic dancer and can follow anyone. She has even picked up some instructing gigs in the past. I've had visions before of the two of us performing on stage before I speak at an event, but I never could understand the visions. I mean, a mother and daughter dancing the Western swing doesn't exactly open a women's conference. Or does it? Who knows where God will take this, but I know that I've had the vision of opening a speaking event with a dance.

Maybe God will invite Beth to this party? She will be shocked when she sees how He reveals His glory through my fifty-year-old body. I hope to usher in His presence in such a way that the atmosphere changes in the room. I read yesterday in Janet's book that "Dancers are atmosphere changers." I agree! Kimberly says in her book, "Even the very word, *dance*, when spoken, carries a lingering sound and implies something is about to happen. It implies that something is about to manifest. It is a word that commands but is inviting. Say the word three times, and you will understand. It encourages connection and purity. It requires and demands authenticity." Try it. *Dance, dance, dance.* Can you feel the energy?

Both of these books are fantastic resources for learning the responsibility of being a Kingdom dancer. Whoa! There's a new phrase: *Kingdom dancer.* I don't think I've uttered those words together ... ever!

Chapter 5

Covenant People
Saturday, October 15-Day 102

Y 'all, when God speaks, listen! I mean, *really* listen. Today, I experienced rejection in His name. Not by Him, but because I was proclaiming His Word. I had been invited to speak at a conference a few weeks ago. This conference claims it is "here to teach, inspire and empower. Our healing begins when we are able to share our stories. When we know we aren't alone, we can breathe again." It goes on to say that it "is a safe virtual space, for women only. Shame and judgment are not welcome here." Sounds like a great place to share about our purpose and our God who doesn't shame us, doesn't it?

Well, I guess this all-inclusive conference doesn't include Jesus, which in my heart doesn't align. Jesus is the way, the truth, and the life. There is no other way to be inclusive in the conversation.

> *Jesus told him, "I am the way, the truth, and the life. No one can come to the Father except through me."* John 14:6

I also know in my heart that my calling is to speak to "dry bones"—to God's Covenant People. In the New Testament, these are people who believe Jesus died for their sins. I knew going into this conference that they believed in all types of "higher powers," but I felt that I'd be allowed to share just like everyone else. I began speaking, and after only a few minutes into the presentation, the host ended my live session and came back to explain that by sharing scripture, I might "trigger" someone who has experienced religious abuse. I reminded her of the disclaimer I had shared: "I understand at a conference like this there are people from many different faith backgrounds. And we don't have to agree to respect and love one another. My hope is that you will take the principles I share and apply them to your life."

I responded to her shutting me down, saying, "I thought this was an all-inclusive conference." She said it was but that sharing from the Bible would trigger people and that she is trying to set people free from religion. I exclaimed, "Me too!" I told her I wasn't religious and fully understand spiritual abuse. I thought to myself, *Um, yeah, I'm experiencing it now from you, lady!* But truly, I understand religious abuse and how people misuse scripture to paint their narrative. That wasn't what I was doing. I told her I wasn't going to skirt around my message and that I'd gracefully bow out. She thanked me for my time and apologized for wasting it. I let her know that my God wastes nothing.

I guess she forgot that I'm an author and that this would end up in a book. All the good life lessons do! She also apologized for not "doing her homework on me." I reminded her that it was clearly written on the front cover of *Worthy* that it is "A Transformative Bible Study."

Of course, my blood was pumping when I ended our conversation, but I truly wanted to be gracious and show the love of Jesus. As soon as I closed my laptop, God reminded me that these were not "my people." He has called me to witness to those who claim they are living under His new covenant—those who say they have accepted His love and forgiveness and believe that Jesus is the Son of God, who died in our place.

> *After supper he took another cup of wine and said, "This cup is the **new covenant** between God and his people—an agreement confirmed with my blood, which is poured out as a sacrifice for you." Luke 20:22*

Those who proclaim Jesus is Lord but aren't fully embracing the Spirit of God in their lives are the "dry bones" I feel He is calling me to serve. I'm not called to be an evangelist. I'm not called to specifically reach the lost. We each have a unique role in the Body of Christ, and this was God's way of clearly showing me mine. He allowed this to be an object lesson I'd never forget.

Don't get me wrong, I'm praying for the conference host who rejected me, along with her attendees. I pray their eyes will be opened to the Truth, but that is as far as God wants me to go with them. This is part of the freedom and abundance that comes with walking closely with Him. I can let go of what isn't mine and be obedient to what is.

Chapter 6

PREPLANNED
Thursday, Thanksgiving Day, November 24–Day 62

My, how the days get away from us! I wasn't sure if I was going to leave the days in the chapter headings or not until I saw that forty days had passed since I'd last written about this journey. Truth is, I wasn't sure I'd make it back to this book to continue writing it or even follow through with the dance. This encounter with God seemed to have come out of nowhere, and because it is such an enormous stretch for me, I began talking myself out of it.

I've only told two people, Janet and Andrea, and I was justifying in my mind that they wouldn't ever ask about it again or follow up. I'd even reached out to my cousin to ask about flags and workshops and didn't hear back, so I rationalized: *It doesn't really matter if I do this. People are going to think it's silly anyway. I mean, how awkward—"Welcome to my birthday party! Let me perform for you."* (More on the performance issue in Chapter 17.)

But God!

For ten out of the forty days I've been "missing in action" I was on a hiking vacation with Darren. It was a long road trip with plenty of time to listen to music. I thought about my "carpet" encounter and what song might be appropriate for my dance. And because I'm an author and an author coach with books on the brain 24–7, I thought about this book and its word count. I couldn't believe how the words flowed out in the first four days of writing. The more I thought about the encounter and request, the more I saw His hand.

You might be wondering where I stand on the idea of dancing at this point and what the plan is. I'll get to that in just a moment, but let me tell you how good God is first. He plans ahead!

Sometime in September (before the calling), I scheduled a lunch with a friend from my church who oversees our women's ministry. The intention was to discuss the possibility of a mother-daughter event late in 2023. With our busy schedules and my travel, we set lunch for November 10, 2022, knowing we had plenty of time. At lunch, we talked about everything under the sun and then some. I shared my idea for the event, and she excitedly asked if I had heard the theme song for the February women's retreat. She shared a bit about the song and sent it to me as we wrapped up our conversation.

As I prepared to drive away from the restaurant, I started the song. By the first stoplight after pulling out of the parking lot, tears were flowing. The song was powerful. In traffic, I continued and pulled into my next destination before the song ended. I didn't turn it back on when I got back in the truck and don't really recall my thoughts about it until a few days later. After feeling the urge to dance one morning, I chose that song. It broke me. Tears danced down my cheeks while I moved prophetically. The movements poured out so naturally that a song over seven minutes long seemed like a blink of an eye. I pushed repeat and danced again and again.

Having never choreographed a dance, I began to count the beats and capture my thoughts about the movements. I wasn't sure if I'd remember the next day. Unsure of what was even happening or if I would actually dance at my party, I continued as if I would. I'm still not sure what, where, or how, but I know now that God has been planning this for a very long time.

Chapter 7

ROYALTY

Monday, November 28–Day 58

Today, I ordered my tutu and flags. What am I doing? Oh, my! I also updated the countdown in my phone to the date of the actual birthday party we are hosting in San Antonio, Texas.

January 7, 2023, is only thirty-nine days away! My birthday isn't until the twenty-sixth, but we're celebrating early with family. This moves my dance up by nineteen days! I'm freaking out on the inside. Yes, I am!

While praying this morning, God gave me peace about this and reminded me that stretching is uncomfortable. I danced and it felt good, but honestly, I began to feel awkward. It's time to get the flags in so that I can get a feel for them. I'm not sure if I ordered the right flags or not, but I ordered a pair that would get here the quickest. These, I reason, can be practice flags, and then I can order another pair if they aren't what I'm hoping for. This is the peace God provided—the peace of letting go of the details and trusting Him.

I've been searching online for days, trying to coordinate the flag color with the tutu and both with the song. The song I feel God led me to is "Royalty" by Kimberly and Alberto Rivera. This is the song that my friend shared with me, and it is exactly the song for *this* dance on *this* day. God is so creative in how He is pulling all of this together. He is showing Himself in the simplest of ways. My prayer right now is that the tutu and flags are perfect together so that I can focus on finishing this writing, the dance itself, and what He is showing me will come after.

So far this is what I've received: I'm to dance and introduce a new ministry called *A Moved Soul*. This will be a retreat-style workshop, where I'll dance and then lead a class to help women understand their purpose. As I'm writing this, I feel a lump in my throat. This is all a stretch! I'm in the beginning stages of teaching on purpose. I'm writing a course based on *Save the Butter Tubs!*. I've given two keynotes based on the process revealed in the book and have another on the calendar that will cover part of the process.

I see the cover of this book—the back cover even. It looks like a photo shoot is in my near future. It would be amazing if I could get this all pulled together and give a copy of the book to our guests at the birthday party as a favor. I see it all coming together but don't want to fool myself either. I know it is going to be a ton of work to pull this off. But I also know that if God has a plan, He will provide.

He's Done It Before

When I think of the bigger picture here and what God wants to be revealed through this dance and book, it's all about His glory. It's about how He shows Himself *through* us if we are willing to surrender. In my experience, God first shows Himself *to* us. There have been a handful of times I've encountered God in a way that has changed my life. A moment in time that is almost indescribable. I'll do my best to share so that you can see other examples of how God speaks to us and reveals Himself to us. I shared in depth in my first book, *Save the Butter Tubs!*, about wrestling with God for thirty days while on bedrest. He won, by the way. I fully surrendered.

Prior to that, I would say my first experience was when He showed me that He loved me unconditionally and I accepted Jesus as Lord of my life. Visiting the church of family friends, I recall exactly where I was sitting the day I felt a love come over me that I'd never experienced before. God had knocked at my door several times before, and I share a bit of that in *Save the Butter Tubs!*, but this time was different. I welcomed the change and began studying who God is and His Word. The pastor at that church preached using the New Living Translation Bible, and it felt like a conversation with an old friend. I still enjoy reading from that translation, but I also cross-reference many others as I study His Word.

Before I sum up what happens in these encounters, I will share a few more examples.

Shekinah Glory

Years ago, while driving home from work, I prayed to God about an experience some women had at a retreat I attended. I don't recall why I didn't go to this particular session, but I missed what some call Shekinah glory. I was on church staff then, and the Monday following the retreat, I was called to the pastor's office and asked about this experience. I told him what I had heard but that I had not experienced it myself.

I heard the guest speaker had prayed for the presence of God to manifest in a tangible way, and the women in the audience reported being covered in gold dust. I heard many women talking about it throughout the day. My emotions stirred, and I felt left out. I wasn't sure what to believe because I hadn't experienced it myself. Then, being questioned about the event made me wonder if it were really possible.

On the drive home that day, I pulled into a Home Depot parking lot and began to pray. I asked God to reveal Himself to me in that way. I believed that He could ... and He did! Right there in the parking lot of a big-box hardware store.

When I opened my eyes after praying, my hands were covered in a fine gold sparkle. I was in shock. I questioned my makeup choices for the day. Did I have on sparkles? Nope! As I sat in shock, my hubs called. I didn't want to touch anything as I didn't want to lose the dust from my hands. Answering with one hand, I tried to explain what I was doing. He must have thought I was crazy. I told him I'd be home shortly.

I proceeded to drive home with one hand, keeping one eye on the road and the other on my sparkly hand. The gold began to fade. When I arrived home, I raced inside and grabbed a roll of clear packing tape; I wanted to capture this gold dust. I attempted to pick up the dust from my hand with the tape, and I stuck it into my journal. I couldn't really see any gold on the tape and felt oddly disappointed. I wanted proof to show others. I wanted to validate my experience.

Fast-forward to 2022, when I was recounting this story with my daughter Beth while writing the *Create Your Victory Channel* journal. We were sitting on the couch in her apartment. My husband was sitting in the room with us but not really paying attention. I told her the entire story, and when I lifted my hand to show her how I had prayed and how it was covered in sparkles, there He was again! I showed her my hand, and I'll never forget the look on her face. It was as if I'd performed a magic trick. We both teared up and sat shocked for a moment. I don't recall what we did or said next, but I know that both of these encounters changed me forever.

The First Carpet Moment

I shared with you at the beginning of this book how God asked me to get facedown on the carpet. It wasn't the first time I'd encountered Him there. In 2006, I experienced a wretched depression that left me suicidal. You can read more about that in *Thank God I Didn't Kill Myself* (for release in 2023). For now, know that God rescued me while I was facedown on the carpet, crying out to Him. His voice was so clear at that moment that my entire countenance was changed. Six months of suicidal depression ended in a moment. Don't get me wrong—I had plenty of emotions and trauma to work through, but the darkness had lifted.

The Making of an Encounter

So what do these encounters have in common? First, they were all unexpected. Secondly, they all required faith and obedience. And lastly, they all changed me and the direction of my life forever. I think that is the reason why this new encounter has me so shaken. I know from experience that sometimes God asks you to do something as a means to get you to do something totally different. I shared about this in *Save the Butter Tubs!* when I related starting my T-shirt company to when God commanded Abraham to sacrifice Isaac. Sometimes God asks us to do things to test our willingness, not because He really wants us to go through with it. He wants to see if we trust Him and if we are willing to go to the ends of the earth if He asks us to.

As such, I am obediently taking each step in this new calling to dance prophetically. I'm listening and staying close to make sure He wants me to go through with it all.

Chapter 8

DOCUMENT
Wednesday, November 30–Day 56

This morning, while commuting over an hour to a book signing, I prayed for this book, for this dance, and for all the other books rumbling in my heart and head. Yesterday was supposed to be the release of *Create Your Victory Channel*, but due to some unforeseen circumstances, I pushed it back two weeks. *Ahhh ... breathing space ...* Or so I thought.

This morning, He convinced me during my prayer time that I could not only release (1) *Create Your Victory Channel*, but (2) this book, (3) the journal companion to this book, (4) another book I've been working on for far too long, (5) its journal companion, and then (6) an idea I've had for years for another journal. He said I already have what I need, I just need to pull it all together and focus. I'm getting used to God and His big belief in my abilities, so I didn't question all the other work I have to do in the next six weeks. Instead, I announced on social media that I will release six books in the next six weeks, and I'm ready to build my VIP Book Launch Team. *What?* My head is still spinning.

This is how I know He wants me to write *this* book and create a companion journal for it. If we don't document what God is communicating to us, we won't believe it ourselves or likely remember. While encountering God, we can often feel His presence and His power within us, which allows us to believe that anything is possible with regard to what He is calling us to do.

Later, when we can't feel His presence, we can talk ourselves out of what He is calling us to do. We begin to question if it was really Him to begin with. When I read back over the entry from October 10, 2022, in this book, I can see, almost like an out-of-body experience, the actions of that day. It seems so unreal to me that He would ask me to do such a thing. I mean, I am a writer and a purpose, publishing, and small business consultant, and He's requesting a dance ministry as well. My eyebrows just popped up! I'm questioning but obediently following.

There are a few ways you can confirm a calling is from God and not in your mind. First, does it align with His Word? Second—and this is often the one that causes doubt—is it so big of an ask that we know we can't do it apart from Him? That's what He wants—for us not to be apart from Him.

> *Remain in me, as I also remain in you. No branch can bear fruit by itself; it must remain in the vine. Neither can you bear fruit*

unless you remain in me. I am the vine; you are the branches. If you remain in me and I in you, you will bear much fruit; apart from me you can do nothing. John 15:4–5

Here's the thing: I consider myself a woman of the Word. I want to become more like Jesus. I'm far from perfect, but I know the Perfecter of my faith. I trust Him with my eternity and my *now*. So here we go. Looks like this is really happening.

Oh, and I forgot to mention that my friend invited me to a special women's winter "Encounter" in two weeks. Interesting. I look forward to seeing how God shows Himself this time.

Chapter 9

A Moved Soul
Saturday, December 10–Day 46

I can't emphasize enough how valuable writing down your hopes, dreams, encounters, victories, and prayers is. Since the last time I wrote here, I attended the women's "Encounter." It was everything I could have hoped for. God showed up and reminded me of His timing. The worship team sang a song I had never heard before, *Tend* by Bethel Music and Emmy Rose. One line in the song broke me:

I'll remain in You
You'll remain in me
And I will trust Your timing[1]

I could have left then and been filled, but He had more for me. The speaker used winter as an analogy for our life of producing fruit. She reminded us that even though we don't see the fruit in the snow, God is nurturing those seeds deep in the earth. That's exactly what I feel like is happening with this "fresh" call on my life. It isn't fresh at all. It has just been buried deep in the snow, cracking open as the ground hardened around it. I've been talking to God about this long winter in my journals for years.

In 2013, I journaled:

This crazy dream has taken up root. Well, I guess it was always there and now it is sprouting again. Let's just say it's been a long winter. This seed has been buried in the ice for far too long.

When I start to think back of my most enjoyable moments, they all involved me dancing or being physical. Some of the best feelings I ever experienced were spinning around a dance floor. I remember revealing this to my friend many years ago. On top of the hill where we were chatting, I shared some favorite ballet poses. My friend encouraged me to audition for the Arthur Murray Dance Studio. I did and was hired! I have danced since but never thought that dream would reemerge.

Now that I'm forty and figure I have another twenty years at peak, fifty if I live as long as my grandma, I just don't want to look back in twenty years and regret not giving it my all. I don't know where any of this will lead me, but I know that even just starting with stretches and holds feels amazing.

Today, I wore tights with my skirt to church and about came out of my skin holding back my dance desires during worship. I know I'm out of shape and overweight, but I know with God all things are possible. I know our bodies are amazing, and with proper care, they can bounce back from near death if that's God's will. I see a challenge. I'm not sure how to capture it. It would be amazing to make a show about it. I'd love for it to be my full-time job over the next year! A blog, a book, a documentary? Hmmm ... Oh, the possibilities!

Ten days later—October 30, 2013

I want to wake up and be excited about my work. Be excited about my life. I think something like "project crazy ideas" is not so bad. I know I will continue to have crazy ideas. It's a matter of how crazy! I love my creative, crazy self, but I need an outlet! I need a way to share my wackadoodle self and preferably make some money in the process.

My head spins with ideas and ideas about my ideas. The idea of bunheads and ballet slippers makes me want to be thirteen again. I wish I had never stopped dancing. I wonder sometimes if this obsession is a distraction or if pursing it will bring me to life again. It could be a journey to a new me. A journey unlocking parts of me I forget about. I mean, look back at all the times I tried to go back to dance.

When my friend asked me if I could do anything, I answered, "Dance." After I had James, I went back to it. Then God tells me I will speak wearing a tutu? What? Maybe there is something to that. Maybe? I guess I just need to start and trust the journey. It could make for a really cool book!

God Brings It All Together

As you can imagine, after publishing seven books prior to the one you're reading now, I laughed out loud and under my breath questioned, "Really, God?" when I read those journal entries. Especially the last part about writing a book about it. I'm still shaking my head in disbelief at how God brings it all together.

I headed to my stack of journals to look for the first time the idea of A *Moved Soul* emerged in my life. As with all my creative thoughts and ideas, I document them, and I knew A *Moved Soul* had come to me since moving into this house. I was determined to scour my journals until I found the entry. As I pulled my stack of journals from the top of the closet, this one fell open to the above entry! Prior to reading it, I had no recollection of journaling about this. Or about what I called "The Studio." In 2013, I was dreaming of a place for artists to freely create. I must have been reading Steven Pressfield's book *The War of Art* because I wrote, "A place where people can let their guard down and leave resistance at the door." I wanted it to include a dance studio and a writing studio. Interestingly, this is what I've been thinking about again for the past several months. I'm thankful for the journals, as they help me to see God weaving it all together.

Twenty-seven days from today, I'll be setting up for my fiftieth birthday party at a rental house in San Antonio. My heart is pounding faster just typing that. I hope the ceilings are high enough and the living room is big enough. I did my best to pick a house that would work without letting Darren in on the surprise.

This week, a few things happened. I ordered custom flags—shorter and in the specific colors I saw in the vision. The practice flags are a bit too long, and the colors don't convey the message of the song. I'm trusting God for this ministry idea and felt He approved and provided for the investment. Hopefully, the shorter flags will be better for the indoor space as well. I started working on my tutu as well. I mentioned earlier that I had purchased one, but it wasn't what I had envisioned, so I'm modifying it. I need to wrap up loose ends with the outfit overall, but I'm headed in the right direction.

Sadly, I don't think I can arrange a photo shoot in time to make the book cover and have books in hand for the party, but I'm going to do my best. I have some local resources and may be able to print special editions for the partygoers. We will see how it unfolds as we get closer.

The thing about this deadline, and now the deadline of the other five books, is that God knows what I am capable of more than I do. He is stretching me in every aspect. I have to be more mindful of how I invest my time and energy, of what I'm eating to fuel my body, and of my sleep and recovery, all while staying close to Him. The more I lean in, the more He shows me. The vision becomes clearer, and He reminds me of something from my past that applies to now. Hence, the title of this book, A Moved Soul.

When we first moved to East Texas in 2008, I was struggling to articulate my ministry vision. I came up with the idea of A Moved Soul and purchased the domain name, along with some of those silicone wristbands (popular at the time) stamped with "A Moved Soul." The idea is that you'd be so moved by God that you'd move in response! Move in obedience. It's the response to His very first call to us—"Follow Me." It's a move we have to make. Not just a thought, but an action.

I finally found the journal where A *Moved Soul* first appeared. The entry was from October 2010. With different ideas stirring in my mind, I brainstormed and captured the idea of "moved souls." And then, during a sermon when the speaker mentioned that the best translation of the Bible is our lives, I wrote in all caps, "A MOVED SOUL." Not knowing what I was doing with it then, I'm humbled now to see how God is bringing all the pieces together. Still not sure where God will take this, but I'm taking it one step of obedience at a time.

Chapter 10

Colors Divine
Thursday, December 15–Day 41

C olors are powerful. One of my many crazy ideas is to create a space with different rooms of different colors. Guests can walk through them and document what feelings and memories the colors evoke.

Today, prophetic worship artist Leisl Nicole McCrea, with Spirit Fire Silks, sent me a video of her with my custom-dyed silk flags. I cried. They evoke the exact feeling I was praying for—royalty. She even mentioned that they look like jewels in person. I'm beyond excited and can't wait to receive them. I feel like this is a "hands and feet of Jesus" moment. We truly are the Body of Christ. Leisl used her gifts to provide the tools for me to express mine. I pray that out of my obedience, many will encounter the glory of God in a new way.

As my cousin Janet shared in her manual, choosing the right color for your flags is important. While I loved the colors of my first set, I knew they weren't right for the song I feel God is calling me to start with. And as I mentioned before, those flags are a bit long for me. I'm looking forward to receiving the new set and practicing with them.

There are only twenty-two days until my party. I've been practicing daily, even through a sinus infection. (That was tough.) Practice is paying off as my endurance is improving, and I'm falling in love with God all over again.

Chapter 11

Progress Not Perfection
Saturday, December 17–Day 39

Y'all, I came across this writing from 2019 and had to share it! It was an entry for what I thought might become a health journey book. I can't help but laugh out loud with God. Read this long chapter, and I'll catch up with you after this blast from the past.

Monday, March 18, 2019

Why am I having thoughts of this again? Why can't I get this out of my mind? I don't have to be a bikini competitor to be healthy. I don't have to stand on a stage to be acknowledged. Maybe as a Christian author, it would actually hurt my image? I just can't help but look at the before and after pictures and be inspired.

I watch through social media my distant friend Kathy, who I met in 2009 (the last time I felt good about my body). She hasn't stopped. She competed in the World Beauty Fitness and Fashion Transformation Division and earned her way onto the world stage in London.

What have I done in the last nine years? I found all the weight I'd previously lost. I've cried many nights over health issues and feelings of disappointment. Don't worry, I'm not going to have a pity party. I'm sure there will be days ahead where you'll be invited to one, but today is not that day.

Tonight, as my husband sleeps, I dream with eyes wide open. I remember the feelings I had in 1998–99 when I was in the best shape of my life. I had six-pack abs, y'all! I recall a friend asking me what was going on with my stomach when I was wearing a cropped top. She couldn't believe the definition. I recall lying on my side and not seeing my midsection sag toward the bed. Am I crazy to think I could have that again?

Some would say yes. I had already had one child by that point. I gained well over sixty pounds with that first pregnancy and did more than bounce back. I had muscle, a shape I felt good in, and a discipline that has long since run for cover. Now going on nineteen years since my last child ... I can barely get that out. Nineteen years my weight has been out of control. It's been up. It's been down. I've completed four half-marathons and a sprint triathlon. I've hiked more miles than I can count on numerous trips. I've also had too many health scares.

The gene mutations and disorders I've been disagnosed with is not something I enjoy sharing. I will, however, give you a brief list.

I'll start with the ones that are genetic:

- Factor V Leiden—sticky blood

- Factor II—too much fibrin in my blood

- Neurocardiogenic syncope—a fainting disorder

- Other gene mutations that cause me to not be able to properly process B vitamins and certain medications

Then there are the other great issues people can't see, and some don't even acknowledge as real:

- High diastolic blood pressure—the bottom number is high; apparently this is the bad number to be high

- Fibromyalgia—unexplained muscle and nerve pain

- Arthritis—mainly in my knees; I've had knee pain since my teens

- And the most recent diagnosis—the catalyst for this life change—benign paroxysmal positional vertigo (BPPV). It happens when small crystals of calcium get loose in your inner ear. You may feel it when you're getting in or out of bed or tilting your head up. Various studies show people over age sixty are more likely to get BPPV. I'm not over sixty! I just turned forty-six. My grandmother suffered spells of vertigo in her eighties and nineties, which resulted in many trips to the emergency room.

Now mind you, I was recently sick with an ear infection. This could be related. I'm still waiting on my appointment with the ear, nose, and throat doctor. I know there is something going on in there, as my left ear has sharp pains and my right ear sloshes when I move my head upside down.

Needless to say, I'm probably not the best candidate to be jumping into any fitness routine, but I am the candidate who needs it.

I'm not a doctor, a health nut, a scientist, or an expert in the field of fitness or health. I'm just a normal, middle-aged—oh, God, did I really just say that?—woman.

This is my experiment.

Tuesday, March 19, 2019

I can't believe I woke up this morning still excited about this. Last night as I drifted to sleep, I told God that He would have to help me want this and be disciplined enough to follow through, because I have tried so many times and failed.

I can't tell you how many before pictures I've taken. Not this time. At least not as of today. I just want to do this my way and outside of what the world says I should do. Besides, there are plenty of unflattering pictures floating around social media. Of course, I know some tricks to deceive the world into thinking I'm a smaller size (as we all do when posing). But the reality is, you can't hide reality. I'm 211.6 pounds as of writing this.

At this moment, no one knows of this desire I have to be shockingly different in my physical appearance by October. Not even my hubs. I have told no one. I'm not sure what to even say at this point. I don't know if I will compete on a stage. My hesitations are many. First, let's just talk about the size of that swimsuit. Oh, wait … not much there to mention.

Then there is the dreaded fake tan. This milky white skin doesn't tan. I do freckle and have joked for years that one day they would all grow together and I'd be tan. Unfortunately, that's not how it works. Instead, I visit the dermatologist yearly to have spots cut out and burned off. So I ask myself, do I really want to be painted a golden brown or awkward orange? What about my stretch marks? Wrinkles? Oh, the list is long. And then I ask myself, *Is that why I am doing this at all? To compete?*

No. I don't want to compete. I just want to feel incredible again. It's not even about looking in the mirror and liking what I see. I'm so blessed to have a husband who tells me I'm beautiful all the time. I've started to believe him. I think he sees me the way God sees me.

So what are my reasons? You know the saying "Start with the why"? It will get you through the tough times. It will keep you from quitting. My why has to be big enough to carry all 211.6 pounds of me to the gym today. That's a BIG why. I'm not sure what that why is, but I think it has something to do with you. Yeah, you.

I like proving God can do things that people don't think are possible. I also enjoy telling how God carries me through my crazy dreams and ideas. If you've read my first book, *Save the Butter Tubs!: Discover Your Worth in a Disposable World*, you know that God wastes nothing. I don't always do things right or with the proper amount of training, but I love watching how God uses my brokenness.

I'm not promising to do this right either. I don't have a system figured out. I don't even have a plan for this book other than journaling my honest emotions, experiences, and expectations.

In 1998–99, I followed a plan of weight training, cardio, and eating low-carb, low-fat meals. It worked. This time around, I'm not sure what my eating plan will look like other than taking out processed carbs as much as possible.

Here's the deal. I don't like the gym, and I don't like to cook. I do like to hike and ride my bike, but I don't live in a place conducive to either of those activities. But, I will work with what I have, with what I know, and Google the rest.

I know that having a vision, a system, and a deadline will help me reach my goal. Knowing what actions to take each day simplifies the process. In other words, if I can eliminate the guesswork and trust the process, I will make progress.

Today, I woke at 7:00 a.m. and fasted until 10:30 a.m. Then I had a protein shake with two hundred calories. Oh, that's another thing. I don't like counting calories, macros, or tracking my food. What am I even thinking?

This is what I want. I want to find healthy food options that are easy, I can make quickly, and I won't get tired of. I want to find exercises that empower me and make me feel strong. Oh, and I want to look like a bikini competitor in the end ... maybe just without the tan.

So I'm going to head into the kitchen and hope there is a frozen veggie burger still in there, zap it in the microwave, slather some prepackaged guacamole on it, and then head to the gym.

Sometimes people think that because I'm an author, speaker, and coach working from home, I have all the free time in the world. You know that "since you don't have a job" statement that I loathe. I do have a job. I write, speak, and coach. I run my own business. All me. The website, the social media, the marketing, the scheduling—you name it, I do it. Oh, and I work as a publishing coach as well. So if you want to use my situation as an excuse for you not to get your rear in gear, go ahead. That's on you. I will no longer be using excuses.

Instead, I will choose to exalt the Creator of the universe, the Creator of you and me. The One who has given me a spirit of power, love, and self-discipline.

5:00 *p.m.* Made it to the gym. Worked the elliptical for thirty minutes doing high-interval training. Or at least that's what I call my method. I start at level five and warm up for five minutes (sometimes two when I'm in better shape), then increase the intensity by one every minute until I'm at level fifteen. Then I start again at level five.

When I'm in better shape, I sometimes start higher, or at least don't return all the way to five, and often go higher than fifteen. Today, I'm just celebrating that this Tuesday, I was in the gym and not the emergency room.

It felt good to sweat because I was working out versus having a fainting spell. I know talking about sweat is gross. I'm sure it won't be the grossest thing we come across on this journey.

This past Sunday, we left church early because I wasn't sure I was going to make it through without fainting. Remember my neurocardiogenic syncope? Fancy name for "My head and heart don't always talk like they should, and it causes me to pass out." It first started when I was sixteen. It's hereditary. My mom has it. I remember the first time I saw her faint like it was yesterday. Her eyes rolled back in her head, and I thought she was going to die. It was terrifying. I must have been around ten.

Now I sometimes wonder which is worse: feeling like I'm going to faint, and trying to protect my husband from the embarrassment and me from the people who insist my blood sugar is low, or the actual fainting itself. The older I get, the worse the recovery seems to be. And of course, it freaks everyone around me out, and they all want to help. If it ever happens when you're around, just lay me flat on the floor and cool me off. That seems to help. (My head needs to be lower than my legs so the blood can return to my brain.)

So I guess I officially made it through Day One. I even boiled some eggs for dinner. I haven't yet decided on my deadline. It will be at least ninety days, which puts me at June 17. If by some crazy chance I decide to show my new physique at the competition, it is July 20.

Wednesday, March 20, 2019

I almost quit last night. I know, it's only officially Day Two. This is hard. It's hard to change habits. I was looking at pictures of other women who have or are competing, and I don't know if that is good for my overall image. Then I asked myself, *Why am I doing this again? Is it just to compete?*

No, more than likely because of my position in my church and the direction I see my career headed, I don't see this aligning. But you never know how God can use this. I will choose not to get caught up in the details of an outcome that hasn't even happened. I have a good ninety days to consider if I want to put myself out there in that way.

In the meantime, I just need to trust the process. Follow the system. Putting one foot in front of the other and doing the next right thing toward my goal of a healthy, stronger body.

Let's talk just a moment about the crazy scale. So yesterday was my first official weigh-in. I was 211.6. This morning, I was 208.8. That's almost three pounds!

Now let me tell you what I know about those three pounds. I know that 3,500 calories equals a pound. I also know that sixteen ounces equals a pound. So I'm not a fool to think I lost three pounds of fat in one day. I didn't burn 10,500 calories, nor did I reduce my calorie intake by that much or even half.

I did actually track my calorie intake yesterday. Do you want to see what my Day One looked like? I know that whenever I read stories about someone making a dramatic change, I always want the details. I'm not saying I'm going to track and share each day with you, but here was my first day.

Breakfast: Protein shake (two scoops)—210 calories

Lunch: Spicy black-bean veggie burger, covered with store-bought guacamole (I buy the mini pre-portioned ones. Don't hate. I know they aren't good for the environment. One step at a time here, okay,) and a cup of cauliflower rice stuffing (again store-bought, freezer section)—270 calories

Afternoon snack (right after the gym): Two hard-boiled eggs with pink salt—154 calories

Dinner: My special egg salad (This is how I make deviled eggs too, but I toss it all in a bowl and call it a salad: two hard-boiled eggs, real bacon bits, sour cream, shredded cheese mashed all together.) and for dessert, an Atkins® lemon bar—509 calories

Total calories for the day: 1,143, and according to my Fitbit, I burned 2,296 by existing and the little gym trip.

As you can see, I'm sure this wouldn't make the health cookbook of the year, but it worked. It worked to keep my calories down and keep me full. I will most likely repeat the same menu today and maybe flip dinner and lunch. Who knows?

Right now, I'm fasting as long as I can. There is a fancy term for this called "intermittent fasting." Look it up. From my understanding, it basically gives my body a chance to use some of the stored calories for fuel. I have seen many people use it with great success.

I've never been a fasting type of person. I've always been the type who eats breakfast first thing in the morning. Honest moment: sometimes thinking about what I was going to eat for breakfast is what got me out of bed. Raise your hand if you've been there. Okay, since I can't see your hand, let me know on social media. Let's be cryptic, and you can just tag me in a post that says, "Raising my hand." Everyone will wonder. It will be great. Seriously, do it.

On the agenda for today, a leg workout. Now with my ear issue (remember that BPPV?), I can't bend over, so there will be some exercises I can't do until it heals. Today will likely include some glute kickbacks on the machine, some leg presses in the weight room (which means getting to the gym before it gets packed), calf raises on the machine, and abductor/adductor hip and thigh exercises on the machine.

I enjoy working my lower body because it's stronger than my upper body. What I don't like:

my knees. They creak, crack, and hurt. Squats aren't in my repertoire for this reason. This is also the reason I'm not a prima ballerina. Well, that and a few other reasons, but that would be a dream come true. I love dancing. Unfortunately, this ear–BPPV thing doesn't allow for spinning. I spin without spinning.

But seriously, if I could go back in time, this is what I would have trained for. I love ballerinas. I love their long, lean, perfectly controlled limbs. Don't even get me started on tutus. I would wear one every day if I could. There may be a time in my old age when I do just that.

When I first started speaking publicly, I wanted to be free of the standard professional suit and dress in a way that would become my signature. I prayed about my style and what I should wear on stage. I'll never forget when God said, "A tutu." I was like, *What? Are you kidding me?* Even as I type this, I think this may very well be a thing that happens again in the future. Yes, I said *again*. It did happen.

I spoke to a group of fourth-graders in my dear friend Tina's class. Tina and I have been friends since our freshman year of high school. She knows my crazy. I was speaking to the students about the career you think you want and how it aligns with the skills you have. A tutu was appropriate. I wanted to be a ballerina, but I didn't possess those skills.

All was fine and dandy until the fire alarm went off. I looked at Tina as she was instructing the students and questioned, "What do I do?"
In Tina fashion, she replied, "You get in line," as if I should remember what to do in a fire drill.
"Where are we going?"
"To the playground."
You've got to be kidding me. I'm a five-foot, eight-inch woman wearing pink tights and a tutu. Now I get to stand on the playground in front of the entire school.

Oh, the adventures I get myself into! Be careful what you ask God; remember, the tutu was His idea. The reviews I received on the program from another teacher made it all worth it. She said she wished they'd had someone speak about career alignment when she was in school.

Who knows, maybe that's why God wants me to get in shape? He wants me to don that pink tutu again. Truth be told, I'd be glad to. I loved talking to those kids. I even made up a game with these big fuzzy dice to get them dreaming about what was possible for their future.

I wonder where those kids are today. I wonder if they remember the lesson I shared.

That's the thing about our lives—we never fully know the impact we are making on those around us. I talk about this in chapters 14 and 15 of *Save the Butter Tubs!*. If you haven't read *Save the Butter Tubs!*, let me just tell you that you have great influence on the people you encounter, and we should all be more intentional about showing kindness and love.

You've probably heard the analogy of our life as a tapestry that we only see from the back, with strings going every which way. But one day, we will see the front. We will see how it all comes together. Oh, what a glorious day that will be! Not because we will see how our lives come together, but because that will be the day we meet our Creator face to face.

Thursday, March 21, 2019

Whomp, whomp, whomp. That's how I feel about yesterday. It wasn't as bad as it feels in my head, but I didn't make it to the gym. I did walk two miles with the hubs around our neighborhood, but before you think that was a great feat, know that we do this all the time. It may be healthier than nothing, but it certainly hasn't helped me reach my goals. Hubs would say the same, and he walks way more than I do because he has an active job.

As a writer, my activity comes in spurts. There will be days when I only walk to the bathroom and the kitchen and back to my office. Then there are days when I am running errands or meeting clients and adding a few more steps in. Either way, steps alone aren't doing it.

My eating may be helping, however. I am down another pound this morning. Yesterday, I was able to fast until 11:00 in the morning. While my calories were over my goal of 1,200, I landed at 1,591. I can't imagine what it would have been had I not made an effort to control them or made better choices. I said I wasn't going to track calories, but maybe I should for a while.

One thing I meant to tell you yesterday about the dramatic three-pound drop—in case you've not done any of your homework—your weight fluctuates throughout the day. Another factor to consider is the amount of inflammation we have in our bodies.

Again, I'm not an expert or a scientist, so do your research. I have found this to be true over the years. If I eat certain things that cause inflammation in my body, my weight can do the exact opposite and shoot up three to five pounds overnight.

Inflammation is in the back of my mind as I make some of my fast, easy frozen meals. I try to choose things that don't have artificial colors or flavors. There's just no need for that. Especially dyes. I don't care if my BCAA (branched-chain amino acid) powder makes my drink red, yellow, or green to match the flavor. As long as it does its job, I'm good with whatever color it is. I'm thankful that some of the big players in the food industry are now trying to color and flavor their foods with natural plant-based ingredients.

I know, I know. I should be eating things fresh from the earth ... blah, blah, blah. Maybe someday I will get there, but right now, it's about small changes that work with me and my lifestyle.

Let's discuss why we so often fail at eating better or changing our habits. We try some extreme shift, like throwing out all of the bad food—and by *bad*, I mean canned goods, boxed food, and pretty much anything that didn't get plucked straight from the earth and into your fridge. That is not the solution. How long is that going to last for someone who doesn't like to cook at all or doesn't like to shop often? Let's take cilantro, for instance, one of my favorite flavors on the planet. It doesn't stay fresh long. I have tried wrapping it in paper towels, and that seems to help but not much. So I can only buy a small amount at a time. Thus, I'm back at the store and being tempted by other things I don't need. It's this horrible cycle.

So I'm starting with small changes. Small things I can easily manage. A system that works for me. It may not work for you. Shoot, it may not work for me. I'll let you know in ninety days. So what's my system? My system is eating low to no carbs, intermittent fasting, and exercising, which includes weight training and cardio.

I'll let you in on the details as I can or feel I should. I'm not writing this to end up being one of those Instagram stars, showing "befores and afters" or pictures of my backside. I will admit, I did that once. I was wearing leggings and took before and after pictures. I was trying to lift my rear back to where it was twenty years ago.

I did make some progress but didn't feel I was supposed to share those pictures with the world. I don't feel that is my calling. I do love looking at the befores and afters of others, if they are tastefully taken. It's inspiring to see how people can transform themselves.

My goal: to wear the same dress I wore last October to a conference again this year but have it dramatically taken in. That to me would be an amazing before and after. There is a picture of me speaking on stage in my beautiful dress—so gorgeous I literally cried the day I bought it. I was so excited. But when I look at that picture, I want to cry for a different reason. It was supposed to be one of the happiest days of my life, speaking about my newly published book, but I didn't feel confident in my own skin.

I've given myself grace. That was a big year of learning so many new things at once. This year, no mercy! Well, except for God's. Thankfully, His are new each morning. So instead of feeling down about not hitting the goal I had in my mind for yesterday, I will rejoice that I made better choices than last week and did lose a pound.

I will rejoice in the conversation I had with my husband as we walked yesterday. We have several hiking trips planned for this year. The first one is in thirty-five days. I told him I won't be partaking in any unhealthy food between now and then, except on Easter, which is only four days before the vacation. I'll celebrate that one day and move on to my goal.

Then while on vacation, I'm sure I will allow myself some leniency but remember that I have a ninety-day goal. I need to use that trip as a fun exercise opportunity and stay on track as much as possible. I even hate typing that. *Stay on track.* What does that even mean? I want to fuel my body and honor it with things that make me feel good long term, not just for that moment. I want to enjoy the freshness of fruit, not the sweetness of processed cake.

I'm going to go somewhere that is sketchy territory. Before I met my husband, I didn't eat many sweets. I would have desserts at holidays and occasionally a candy bar or some such treat. I was much more of a savory eater. Still am, but now I consume more desserts. My husband has a sweet tooth. Actually, I think all of his teeth are sweet. He loves sweets and can eat things that usually make me sick to my stomach with their richness. Thus comes the temptations. If he's indulging, I indulge. If he brings it in the house, I will likely partake.

Now, hear me LOUD AND CLEAR: I'm NOT blaming my husband for my weight issues. I have just let myself pick up habits that I didn't have before. Now it's time to turn the tables. He is willing. He is giving up sweets for a twenty-one-day fast we are doing at church, starting at the beginning of next month. He has also agreed not to bring anything unhealthy into the house for the next ninety days.

The crazy part is, I know his weight will melt like butter and shedding mine will take a concerted effort. Why is that? Well, men have more muscle mass, and carrying around more muscle means burning more calories. Hubs also gets more steps with his job, remember? Not that this is at all a competition with my hubs to see who can lose the most or the fastest. It's just one more thing that can get me down during this process.

I'm just happy that for now, we are on the same page. When I lost thirty-two pounds back in 2009–10, I was pretty much on my own. He wasn't interested in calorie-counting or exercising over and above what he was already doing, between our walks and his work. With that said, this should be easier.

No matter what, I need to do this for me. Like I said in *Save the Butter Tubs!*, "Growing up, my life motto was, 'It's my life. If all those around me died tomorrow, it'd still be my life, and I'll have to live with the decisions I've made.'" God forbid my husband die. The point is, I have to be happy with me, for me. I go on to explain that after giving my life to Christ and understanding that in the end, I answer to Him, I changed my motto to "My life belongs to Christ. If everyone around me dies tomorrow, are my decisions going to be pleasing to Him?"

You see, often we make idols out of the best things in our lives—our spouses, our kids, and our families. We need to fully surrender to God. The best thing about surrendering is that He will help us through even our battles with weight. Being overweight, overeating, and overindulging in *relaxation* isn't the abundant life He talks about.

On that walk last night with hubs, he said he'd been praying about his appetite and had seen a change over just a few days. I love that we are on the same *track*.

Saturday, March 23, 2019

Creating a new routine is hard. I know it works. I just need to do it. I haven't been back to the gym all week. Thursday night, I did walk another two miles with the hubs, but yesterday, nada. In less than a week, I'm struggling.

Hubs and I did go to the grocery store yesterday evening. I can't let him go alone because he always returns with something he shouldn't. I picked up some of my go-to easy items, and hubs was on board. I think he misses the times when I used to cook more. I told him that maybe when I got some of this extra weight off, I'd feel more like it.

I should be praying about it. Being empty-nesters makes it even harder for me. I wish I had inherited my grandma's love for cooking. I really just don't enjoy it and usually grumble when I have to prepare something to take somewhere. Maybe it's because I'm not that skilled at it. I don't know. I do know that I'd rather spend my time doing something I enjoy, and currently cooking isn't one of those things.

There are shortcuts for food and meal prep, but I haven't found any shortcuts to working out. The stomach bug doesn't count! And God knows, I am not that desperate to get the weight off that I'd trade my health to be thin. The whole point is to improve my health.

Today, our plans are to visit the grandbaby for a couple hours and then have game night with some friends this evening. I have some work to do in the office this morning, I will spend my appointment with the King, and I will do a bit more writing on two other projects. Then it will probably be time to head out. Maybe I need to rearrange the order of things. For now, writing first thing is most productive for me. Before my head is clogged with worldly noise. I also know, however, that I can write after my hour with the King and be just as productive, if not more so. That is how I wrote my last book. Worship time was always first thing, ushering in His presence.

I'm not sure what will change, but I know that in order to stick to the system and meet my goal—which is officially NOT competing—something has to. God has made it clear that competing is NOT for me, and I'm perfectly okay with that. I don't have to spray myself orange—I mean tan. But if you recall, goals have to have a big enough why. They have to have something that makes you *want* to achieve them, even when we fail or fall short, even when the scale goes up overnight, and even when we don't make it to the gym. Why do we get back up? Why would we push through?

Chapter 12

Follow His Lead
Sunday, December 18–Day 38

A re you still cracking up from yesterday? I am! Can you relate? My intentions were good, but obviously, there wasn't a big enough reason to continue because that was it! Five days to fizzle. Wow, five days! That book was supposed to be titled *Progress Not Perfection*. Fitting since I made five days' worth of progress, if you can count that as progress, before fizzling right out.

Since that time in the late nineties I mentioned with the nice abs, there have been too many starts and stops to count. Before pictures, but never after pictures. Milestones were achieved with half-marathons and a sprint triathlon, but I was still not where I wanted to be, both physically and spiritually.

This, though—this feels different. From-the-depths-of-my-soul different. I can't see the finish line. I thought it would be the birthday party. That would be the day that all of this comes together, and ta-da! I'd be done with this. But that's the thing about encounters—they change you. They beckon you. And they will haunt you forever if you don't take action.

The more immediate the action the better. You'll start to see things unfolding and differently. Experiences from your past will begin to come into focus. Doors will open as if action were the only key. Action is key! But not the only key. We have to stay connected. In order for God to lead us in this dance, we have to be in His arms.

In case you're not a dancer, let me help you understand the intricacies of leading. A slight change in hand position, pressure, or grip can move your partner in beautiful directions. This reminds me of dancing in high school. Every Friday and Saturday night, I'd go to the Bluebonnet Palace in Schertz, Texas. I'd dance and dance. Everything from the waltz to the two-step, from polka to swing—you name it, I'd do it. I could follow, but I can also lead, and I taught my kids to dance from a young age.

I love to be led by someone who can really feel the music. Lead long enough, though, and it is hard to follow someone else. I didn't know this dancing metaphor was going to be so powerful, but it truly is. Think about it. Are you having trouble letting God lead you? It's because you've never been taught how to follow. If you're like me, you've had to lead. You've had to figure out this dance for yourself. (At least that's what the world tells us to do.)

Back to the Bluebonnet Palace. There was a boy who was an incredible dancer. Like a controlled tornado, we'd scoot across the dance floor, gathering eyes. We were good, and people noticed. Sadly, I don't even remember the boy's name, but I remember clearly the time he released his grip on me. I flung off the tips of his fingers into the tables and chairs. It wasn't pretty, but it remains a valuable lesson about holding on to the one who is leading you.

Cling tightly to Him. Far too often we clutch our pride, possessions, grudges, and a slew of other unhealthy habits and things. Let me pull a Dr. Phil here and ask, "How's that working for you?" It hasn't ever worked for me.

My fulfillment and true joy come when I'm clinging to God. Walking with Him. Jesus said, "Follow Me." That is where the fulfillment is. *Follow.* The closer we follow, the easier it is to hear Him whisper. The closer we follow, the more we can feel our position change as He guides us. Your soul knows. Your ego is just trying to talk you out of it. You'll feel it in your heart, your body. If you want to truly feel alive, you've got to go for it. Trust Him and follow His lead. Wherever and however crazy it may seem.

Crazy may seem to go against everything you've been taught. We've been taught that we need to be "normal." What does that even mean? To me, crazy is the unimaginable. It's the things we don't think are possible becoming possible.

Have I mentioned arthritis? Well, I have it. Mostly in my knees and my middle finger on my right hand. As I type, my finger is swollen like a sausage. It looks like they transplanted one of my dad's fingers onto my hand. But it doesn't hurt right now. It doesn't hurt when I hold the flags as they sway in worship to our Creator. My body knows. You'll know. When I'm doing what I'm called to do, when I'm following His lead, time slips away, pain dissipates, and impossible becomes possible.

I actually feel bad sometimes that I'd rather write than go on vacation. Hubs loves to plan trips, and I love to go on them. We have been to some beautiful places and seen God's glory through creation time and time again. But for me, that's not fulfilling. It's lovely but not fulfilling. IYKYK (if you know, you know). I'm sure that to many I sound like a spoiled wife. I'm aware that not everyone can take vacations. I'm aware that I have a fabulous husband, and I'm blessed that he loves to travel and take me places. But if you know, you know. There is a difference between fulfillment and pleasure. While you can have pleasure in fulfillment, experiencing pleasure doesn't mean there is fulfillment.

Did you catch that nugget? Here's another. When you follow His lead, you're off the hook for the outcome. He's only asking you to do *your* part. He's not asking you to create an outcome. This should release all the control freaks from fear. I know it helps this recovering control freak. It allows me to be free. Free from the opinions of others. Free from figuring it out. Wouldn't you like to be free from the feeling of always having to figure things out? Be free!

Now back to the dance ... When you are being led by someone else, you are not determining the next steps. You are not thinking about the music and where it's taking you. You're leaning in, holding on, and moving where you are guided. Doesn't that sound much easier than trying to figure it out? Just lean in, hold on, and move where you are guided!

This is fulfillment—moving where you are guided with ease and grace. You'll end up in places you never thought possible and possibly places you've never even dreamed of. You'll feel His hand—His presence. And with His presence comes peace, joy, love, kindness, goodness, faithfulness, patience, gentleness, and self-control. He's got you. You can relax and move when He moves, where He moves.

Chapter 13

Avoid Heartbreak
Thursday, December 29–Day 27

Yesterday, as I asked Darren about last-minute party invitations, I told him we had two weeks. He corrected me and said it was only one week until my party. With a lump in my throat, I quickly corrected him, "A week and a half."

The party, as I've mentioned, is taking place on the seventh, and I don't actually turn fifty until the twenty-sixth. I'm only rushing the celebration to combine Christmas and my mom's birthday all in one. Yes, Christmas has officially come and gone, but not for my San Antonio family. I'm still wrapping gifts for them! That celebration will happen on the eighth, which is actually my mom's birthday. Same birthday as Elvis, if you care.

As I write this today, I know this manuscript should be wrapped up soon if it's going to make it to editing and print in less than a month. That's a tight turnaround. The lump in my throat—it's still there. It doesn't seem like my fingers can type fast enough. Heavier than usual, they pound the keys as I well up with tears. What am I doing? Is this really even happening? Yes, yes, it is. At least I'm preparing as if it is. If God is just testing my obedience like He did with Abraham when asking him to sacrifice Isaac, I'm okay with that. It lets me off the hook for the big day. I've done my part. I've shown Him I'm willing to follow His lead. And if He wants me to go through with this, I will put on the tutu and move to the music, gracefully (I hope) waving the silky teal and plum-colored flags in front of my friends and family.

Retrospection is a gift. Because I have seen how God moves and works in ways I never dreamed of, I know He can do it again. I may not know what my future holds with regard to prophetic dance, but I do know that God's plans are greater than mine. I also am very aware of what hesitation can do to your mind, body, and soul.

In my book *Save the Butter Tubs!*, I wrote about creative avoidance and how I creatively avoided writing for so long. I didn't lean in. I didn't trust God for the outcome. Not in the beginning. And it cost me. It cost me time, energy, and wellness. Because of my disobedience, my grandma never held a finished copy of that book in her hand. Let that break your heart. It breaks mine.

Who will miss the blessings if you don't take action now? Because I know the cost of disobedience, I understand the reward of obedience. That is what this entire book is really about. As Nike would say, "Just do it." Nike is on to something here. Taking action is biblical. In James 2, we are told, "We are shown to be right with God by what we do, not by faith alone." James goes on to say in chapter 4, "Remember, it is sin to know what you ought to do and then not do it."

You might be reading this thinking, "Okay, great. He talks to you, but I don't know what I'm supposed to do." Stop it! Stop it, right now! You know you are to read His Word. Start there. Stay there. From there, He will guide and move you. If you want to have an encounter with God that moves you, you first have to show up! It really is that simple.

Go back to the beginning of this book. It started with me in prayer. Not at a fancy temple in an exotic city. Not wearing certain clothes. I was walking away from my prayer chair, aka massage chair, and I just talked to God. He responded. I responded. He responded. I responded. He provided vision. He provided clarity along the way. With each action I took, He provided for the next step. He responded to my response. In case you aren't familiar with healthy relationships, this is what one looks like.

We tend to have a distorted view of God based on our earthly relationships and that is why it is vitally important to lean into Him. Allow Him to lavish you with the unfailing love His Word promises. Following Jesus is not just a get-out-of-hell-free card. It is an abundant life of growth through stretching, responding in obedience, and receiving the gifts our gracious God wants us to receive.

What if one day, the thing that has been on your mind, the thing you felt God calling you to, all the ideas

... what if they just disappeared? How would you feel then? We should be thankful that God doesn't stop speaking to us because we stop responding to Him. You have a divine spark; don't limit yourself. God can do all things! Trust Him. You were not given a spirit of fear. Live in the freedom you were given!

Chapter 14

Torturing Yourself and Stifling the Spirit

Tuesday, January 3—Day 23

W ho knew coming up with the subtitle for this book would be so difficult? Well, I sort of knew. Subtitles are tricky. You want to give enough information to help readers make a decision about the book, but then there's a temptation to be cute or sassy. Well, just in typing the word *temptation*, I remember that temptations aren't from God, so let's go with practical—I need a practical subtitle.

I want people to understand the importance of taking action after encountering God. If we don't take action, we begin to torture ourselves. Whether we realize it or not, the disobedience stirs in our soul. It is clearly because we are sinning. Yep, I said it. God tells us in His Word not to stifle the Holy Spirit, but that is what we are doing when the Spirit calls us to move and we dig in our heels.

The original sin in the Bible—you know, back in the garden?—was disobedience. Look at the impact that disobedience has had on the world. That alone should rock our souls! Disobedience matters. If God is whispering in your ear, listen and respond!

What-iffing ourselves to death is not what we are called to do. Second-guessing—nope, that's not it either. Follow! Follow! Follow!

Which leads me to the subtitle for this book: *Boldly Responding to Encountering God.*

Less than a week out from revealing this encounter, all I can do is follow. Overthinking, worrying, or stressing isn't going to serve me well or produce fruit. My go-to torture device is "separation." When I feel overwhelmed by a situation or calling, when I can't "figure it out," paralysis sets in, and I withdraw from God. It's that creative avoidance I spoke of that I allow to come between me and the Creator of the universe. It's like I'm rehanging the veil. What I'm saying is, "Thanks but no thanks." I'm saying, "I don't trust You enough for this." I'm saying that I want to be God and know all the answers before moving forward. Ouch! Am I stepping on any toes yet?

Instead of asking, "Who am I that God could use me in this way?" we should do an ego check and ask, "Who am I to question how God can use me?" And if I'm honest, I'll let you know that this is easier said than done. But my goal is to move through this cycle of questioning as quickly as possible and get on with the act of obedience. To boldly respond ...

Questioning is a normal human response that we see again and again in scripture. But then we also see action. We've got to shorten the time between the call and the action. From experience, I can tell you that it is easier to move in the Spirit. It may feel foreign at first. You may feel like you are having an out-of-body experience. This is a good sign! Get out of the way of what God is doing. Trust me when I say that there is no reason to torture yourself with questions or worse, all-out disobedience.

With just a few days until the party, there won't be a book to hold. I could torture myself with disappointment, but instead I'm learning and leaning. God isn't done with this book. When He is, it will be clear. So I'm planning to print a poster-sized cover image on a foam board to display. That is, of course, if I get the images in time and can pull it all together.

In the meantime, I'm choosing to trust.

Chapter 15

God Is in the Details
Thursday, January 5–Day 21

I didn't sleep well last night waiting on photos for the cover. Nothing like waiting until the last minute! Today is the last day I can get the cover poster printed without Darren seeing it. It's also the last day for me to dance before the party. Strangely, none of this seemed real until I saw the images.

The file link was waiting in my Facebook message inbox this morning. Jamie, my gifted photographer from JME Studios in Tyler, Texas, did an amazing job capturing the emotions. For the cover, I wanted to evoke movement. We did try a few of my initial ideas during the shoot, but ultimately I received exactly what I envisioned, along with beautiful images to use on the back cover and to give my website a facelift. My socials will be popping with some of these soon too. Once the cat is out of the bag, it will be so fun to share all of these.

This morning, as I was designing the mockup cover for the reveal at Saturday's birthday party, I began to feel ill. Almost faint. I wasn't sure if it was the lack of sleep or if God had brought me as far as He wanted and this was His way of saying to stop. I prayed and prayed some more. I cried. I cried out to God. I cried out to my sweet prayer warrior Andrea. We use a video app to communicate regularly since we are in different time zones, which enables us to keep up with each other. At the point of typing this, I'm not even sure she's had a chance to see it, but I *know that I know* that God heard my cries. I pressed on and completed the cover design.

I requested a bit of feedback from Amanda (my business partner, who I also let in on the secret since she won't be at the party) about a last-minute title change. Thank you, Amanda, for your advice to keep it as it is supposed to be: A *Moved Soul*. During this—what I now know to be spiritual warfare—I thought maybe it should be *Moved Souls*. You see, I want it to be about *you*, my readers, seeking encounters and moving in response. Amanda reminded me that it is a memoir and that A *Moved Soul* was appropriate. I agree. It's not all about me but about how God has moved my soul! I'm sharing this calling process out of obedience and as an example of what He can do if we will just get out of His way. I want you to claim the title A *Moved Soul* for yourself.

Confirmation on the title didn't stop me from feeling sick to my stomach. I felt dizzy. I don't recall ever feeling like this before. Words can't adequately describe what was happening. I felt so bizarre. I pulled out all my tricks: got in the massage chair for fifteen minutes, returned to the carpet for prayer, danced with what was by this time a full-blown migraine, then showered, because my mom always says washing your face after a good cry makes you feel better.

By the time I got out of the shower and began dressing for the day, the spiritual warfare was over. God won! He always does. I felt like a completely different person. Almost giddy with peace and empowered like never before, I understood how prophetic dance is a natural extension of my ministry to speak truth and awaken dry bones. It is a doorway to truth so powerful and to the presence of the Lord. Dance truly does change the atmosphere.

After my shower, I popped on my "Uplift" playlist, and the first song was called "Well Done," by Moriah Peters. Those lyrics nailed the moment!

> *I'm headed down this narrow road*
> *Chosen by the few*
> *And all that I know is*
> *You told me to follow You[2]*

I'm still in awe of how God works and of what He did today. This entire journey has been so intimate and powerful. I can't wait to share it with you. I'm committed to staying in the moment during the next forty-eight hours. I won't get ahead of myself or allow the way I think others will react to distract me from what God is speaking to my soul.

God was in the details to get the right flags here the Saturday before the Monday photo shoot. He opened up JME Studios on Jamie's day off to squeeze me in. He helped me get home before Darren that day to keep this between Him and me. And here He is again, sliding the images in at the final moment, with the provisions in place to design and print the cover in time. I'm in awe ... as we should be daily. He is consistently in the details of our lives—we just don't give Him credit.

Chapter 16

CONFIRMATION
Friday, January 6-Day 20

T oday, I woke up to a different message. A sweet confirmation from an old friend who is journeying with me through *Create Your Victory Channel: 365 Journal Prompts to Capture the Goodness of God*. She even shared pictures of her entry for yesterday. Kathryn will be at the party, and I can't wait to share with her just how much her message meant and how God used it to confirm moving forward. Not that I needed additional confirmation at that moment, but I'm sure between now and tomorrow evening, I will!

I'm praying it won't be awkward to gather everyone in the living room to share this story and then dance. Do I share the book cover before or after? Will the ceilings be high enough for the flags? Oh, the questions want to swirl, but I'm stopping them with this confirmation and yesterday's.

I still can't believe the night-and-day difference I felt. God's peace filled my soul, but not to a stillness—to a new energy. My migraine was gone, with no migraine hangover (IYKYK). It was as if He took me by the hand and said, "Here is your to-do list for the day. Get on with it, and leave the enemy behind."

As I type this, Darren is driving us to San Antonio. I'm holding back emotions. Tears of joy, giddiness that I wouldn't be able to explain, and an adoration that makes me want to belt out all these worship songs playing on the radio. I wonder if he has any idea. I've done my best to keep it all a secret. Yesterday, I almost blew it with the poster, though. I thought I ordered a size that would fit in my suitcase. When I picked it up, it was larger than I expected, and it's on foam core so it can't be rolled.

But God in all His glory reminded me of my enormous suitcase, which up until that moment I hated. It's too big to fly with! Once at the airport, I had to take things out of it because it was too heavy. It wasn't even full—just heavy with books. (Pro tip: don't travel with too many books.)

Anyway, it worked out that Darren was resting when I got home from running my errands, so he wasn't aware of what I was up to. I pulled the larger suitcase from the shed and put the poster inside before taking the suitcase in the house. I quickly stuffed it with my other belongings, burying the poster, along with my tulle skirt for the dance. I pray it isn't banged up when I get it out!

Darren later asked why I was taking such a large suitcase for only three nights. I played it off as necessary to fit gifts for my family, a blanket, and my pillow. Since I sometimes overpack, he didn't question any further.

Flags are packed, along with my dance outfit, new Bluetooth speaker, and those old baby-blue wristbands I had made when I was dreaming up A *Moved Soul* almost a decade ago. I'd certainly had no idea it would end up like this. A book title? Nope. A new prophetic dance ministry? Nope. Only God can put those pieces together.

It's hard to be speechless and write a book at the same time. This is why you have to experience God for yourself. I don't think the greatest writers on the planet could pen the encounters of God in a way that someone who isn't having the experience would understand. Like I mentioned earlier, if we don't write it down, we won't remember it moments later. We must capture the words and emotions when the Spirit speaks, because when He doesn't, doubt always wants to. God is often silent after He speaks through such encounters. He is waiting on your response. There is nothing else to say. He told you what to do; now He expects you to take action.

Don't worry if you're not a writer. There are other ways to capture the energy from the encounter. Writing is my preferred method, but I also love video. Sharing with Andrea yesterday allows me to go back and see that night-and-day difference I mentioned. In the first video, I was choked up with tears. The second video I sent her captures the joy and radiance that only the Lord could provide. However you choose to express your encounter, it reminds me of the Morgan Harper Nichols song, "Storyteller":

Looking at old photographs
I'm remembering
You were right there
And You have been ever since
With every page that turns
I see your faithfulness[3]

When I review the past three months, I can't help reflecting on His faithfulness. He truly wastes nothing. The little girl who dreamed of being a ballerina will be dancing in a tutu tomorrow evening in front of her closest family and friends. He brought all the pieces of what seemed like a disjointed and broken life into a beautiful worship experience. Even bigger than a one-time worship event—a new ministry. I still don't know what it will all look like, but I am trusting Him. Each time I lean in, He shows me a bit more. With each step of faith that I take to move toward Him and what He is asking of me, He provides.

I'm looking forward to the next time I open this book to write. I'm not sure I'll have a chance tomorrow, so it will likely be either late evening after the party or on Sunday. Either way, I can't wait to update you on what happens at the party and what I feel is next.

He has already shown me the next two books in what He has named *The Worth Pursuing Series*. One will be a guided journal and the other a Bible study. I've begun work on both and hope to have them out in the first half of the year. Here's another example of how God is in the details and orchestrating what we can't yet understand. When I was mapping out the next two series, I always thought the order would be first *The Worth Knowing Series* and then *The Worth Pursuing Series*; but through this journey and my questioning why this book should come first, He told me, "It takes action to realize who you really are."

Think about that for a moment. Actually, let's dive in. I am stunned, how for years, I thought it was the other way around. I thought that if I knew *who* I was, I'd know *what* I was to do.

When we first encounter God, He calls us to follow Him. Our awareness that we are sinners in need of a mighty Savior comes through encountering Him. Then we follow and learn more about who we are. Then He calls us deeper, and if we obey, we see more of who we are. Even more exciting is that we start to see His reflection in the mirror.

So here's the takeaway: Just do the last thing He told you to do. If you don't feel He has spoken to you and you're wondering what the first step is, it is following Him. To do that, we need to be in His Word. We won't be able to hear His voice if we don't know what it sounds like. We won't know where He is leading until we can clearly hear Him. The first place He leads any believer is to a relationship with Him.

Chapter 17

WHOA, WHAT A NIGHT!
Monday, January 9–Day 17

G od did it. He really led me to prophetically dance in front of my friends and family at the birthday party. I'm still in awe.

There were many times on Friday and Saturday, while hanging around my sister and daughter-in-law, that I wanted to let them in on the surprise. Then Saturday, my friend who left me that message I mentioned on Friday came early, and I wanted to sneak her into the bedroom and reveal the secret. But God—He kept reminding me that I didn't need their approval or support. I needed to trust in Him and Him alone, and that He is my greatest need in moving forward. He alone is our greatest need. And so, reminding myself that temptations aren't from God, I resisted and relied on Him. I prayed for the timing, and He guided.

I decided when packing for the trip that I would wear my tutu (a long tulle skirt) as my party outfit and then add my leggings underneath just before I danced. Little did I know, but that helped set the tone. I wore a teal midi tulle skirt and a black long-sleeve, fitted T-shirt with my leopard-print TOMS® shoes. I added a simple but sparkly necklace my mom had made and some vintage teal earrings she had given me. My curls were bouncy and loose, but I knew I'd need to pull them up for the dance. I'm also thankful I remembered to remove my glasses so that they didn't slide down my face during the dance.

As the night progressed, dinner was served, cake was cut and eaten, and people naturally began gathering in the living room. On the coffee table that I strategically moved closer to the couch earlier in the day, I set up my laptop to record the dance and my Bluetooth speaker to play the music loud enough for everyone to hear. I placed the mockup book cover, facing away, behind me on the wet bar. (Thank you, God, for providing that space!) I left the flags in the bag until it was time to dance.

Then, I slipped away to add leggings, put my hair up, and take off my shoes. I prayed and asked God one more time if He really wanted this. Imagine telling God He has one more chance to back out! Yep, that was me. He said if you can't be who I created you to be in front of your closest friends and family, you won't be able to continue what I'm asking of you. I surrendered and proceeded to the living room. I invited everyone else in for what I said was a surprise and then let them in on the big reveal.

God is in the smallest of details. Up to that point in the weekend, I had been the only one who wanted the ceiling fan on. Everyone else complained it was too cold, so I left it off for the party. When I was setting up my laptop and other props, I laughed that I didn't have to turn the fan off because it was never on.

I began by explaining much of what I shared at the beginning of this book about my desire to do something fun for my fiftieth. I let them know about my carpet meeting with God and this special call to dance. I choked up a few times as I shared about the goodness of God, all that He has brought me through, and how He is using all of it for His glory. My heart was pounding, but not to the point where I needed to stop or back out. I felt a peace. Encountering God is something I could talk about for hours, so I tried my best to keep it short.

Flipping the book cover around, I explained the title and subtitle, which I believe helped some people understand what was coming. Many of these friends and family members remembered A Moved Soul from the wristbands. I saw smiles and head nods, which were comforting.

I let them know that I wasn't performing for them or for God but rather worshipping Him and inviting them to do the same. I pulled the flags out, and my mom blurted out, "Those are the small ones?" Everyone laughed, as I had mentioned the practice flags being twice as long. The sound of laughter naturally eased my soul.

And then I danced. I worshipped. I choked up a couple of times during the song but held it together. I felt beautiful as I moved through the rehearsed steps and let God lead me through the rest. I was comfortable with the flags and felt they were an extension of me. When it was over, I thanked everyone. They clapped, and many commented how beautiful it was.

After sharing such a big secret I'd kept for three months, my desire to shout from the rooftops was strong. I wanted to let them in on everything He was up to. At least what I knew up to that point.

Some people were encouraging and responsive to what they had just experienced. Some wanted to move on, and others I later found out were confused, including my husband.

He is an introvert, so I imagine the whole event was uncomfortable for him. When I asked him what he thought, he said something about "Here we go down another road ..." I didn't take that as an insult or negatively, but he later said he was confused and thought I was giving up everything else I was working on to do this. I laughed and asked if he'd missed the giant book cover poster. With all the other weekend festivities, I figured we'd have five hours on the drive home to discuss it. I needed time myself to process what had just transpired.

I'm thankful that, while I considered what others would say or think, I didn't allow the fear of that to stop me. I believe this is one of the biggest takeaways—for me and for you—in this whole experience. I actually think this is a huge reason why the church is in the situation it is today. Everyone is so concerned about people's feelings that they don't stop to think about grieving the Spirit of God.

I'm not saying we should be blatantly rude or arrogant when following Christ. I've seen that, and it is *not* well received by anyone, even mature believers. But here's the deal: If we never step out of our comfort zone—out of *their* comfort zone—we will never be in the God-zone! We have to stretch, and we have to stretch those around us.

My second cousin Shelley commented before she left that evening about my willingness to be obedient. I told her it was because I understand the cost of not being obedient. I know that cost firsthand, and I know that first and foremost, it is a sin. I don't want to sin. I do that enough as is in my everyday living, growing, and navigating this broken world. Secondly, I know that what God is calling me to be obedient to is part of His plan. If I'm not obedient, there will be blessings I miss and blessings that others miss, and I will feel the weight of disobedience in my spirit.

I didn't tell the whole story, but I wanted to say to Shelley, "I don't have thirty more days of my life to spend in bed." (My battle with Lyme disease is recounted in *Save the Butter Tubs!*.)

Being raised by an artist mother, Shelley seemed to understand the dance as an act of worship. She said something else that was profound to me as I wrap up this book. (We'll get to the conclusion in a moment, but first, more God details.) I hadn't seen Shelley since my grandmother died, and that was before *Save the Butter Tubs!* was released. Shelley was thrilled to leave Saturday with all three books in *The Worth Saving*

Series. She said her mom would have loved to have been here to celebrate all God is doing.

Little did she know that when I was about eleven years old, I wrote to her mom, my great aunt Myrtle. I had seen the movie *Flashdance* and for some reason thought Aunt Myrtle could be my Hanna. Hanna was the main character Alex's muse and encourager. Aunt Myrtle wrote me back and encouraged me to follow my dreams.

Still shaking my head, I am in awe of how God orchestrates events and the smallest of details. Shelley brought several of her mother's paintings as gifts, three of which now hang in my office. Irises are important to my sister Jenifer and me. It started with my dad, who transplanted irises from his childhood home to ours. Later, Jenifer dug some up to give to me. Now I have a flower bed full, as they love our East Texas red dirt. Two of Myrtle's paintings were the same picture, only in different colors. I, of course, took the yellow irises. Jenifer took the other (I don't recall now if they were pink or white).

The fact that there were two iris paintings, one for each of us, is just God showing off, if you ask me. My aunt Myrtle had no idea where those paintings would end up, but she left instructions to her family, saying that the paintings were to be given away and never sold. Shelley was so thoughtful to bring them as gifts for us. My mom took several home as well. I'm not sure why I feel compelled to share this detail other than God—He is in the details.

This birthday will be hard to top. It was special for so many reasons, and I'll be forever thankful for those who were in attendance and indulged me as I worshipped.

Chapter 18

Spiritual Warfare
Sunday, January 15–Day 11

My post on Facebook today:

Confession time. Launching a book is hard work. Launching a personal book about walking with Christ is even harder.

Spiritual warfare is real and heavy. I'm wrapping up a book God surprised me with on October 10th [this book] along with another book about my life-long struggle with depression. Both need to be written. Both are long overdue.

I'm also sharing about the goodness of God daily as I walk readers through my last release, *Create Your Victory Channel: 365 Journal Prompts to Capture the Goodness of God.*

Let's just say the enemy doesn't like me these days.

So I'm asking for prayer. Please pray for me and against any evil that would derail me. If you'd like to join my launch team, I'd love that, but more than anything, today and in the weeks ahead, I need your prayers. I need our God. He knows.

Under Attack

Y'all, the enemy doesn't like this. He doesn't want us to encounter God, much less tell others about our encounters and how wonderful our God is. If you've never experienced spiritual warfare, let me say this: First, you might not be aware that you did. Second, you might need to take bold action. The enemy loves dry bones and sleepwalkers. He'd much rather me be in the other room watching football with my husband than writing about how mighty my God is.

He will use distractions of all types to slow us down, stop us, make us doubt ... whatever he can do to keep us quiet. Remember back in chapter 14? All that yuckiness was prayed away. God handled the enemy. God handed me peace. If you feel like you're in a battle, you are. Walk boldly in the armor of God, and know that if God allows it, He is going to use it.

Chapter 19

I See It
Saturday, January 21–Day 5

I'll be forever grateful for the overwhelming response to my Facebook post last week and the prayers that came with it. They were felt. A peace came over me this week like I've never experienced. I understand that if nothing else comes from this prophetic dance other than this book and the joy I've experienced up until now, that is enough.

But God ...

He arranged a time for my cousin Janet, the prophetic dancer, to come to town. Her sister, my other cousin, lives nearby, and Janet was coming to visit her. She had a gift to bring to me and agreed to bring her various flags for me to try out. Who knew there were so many? The real gift turned out to be us dancing together and her teaching me a few things. She prayed over our time together and showed me the different flags, and I showed her mine. Then she asked me to dance to "Royalty".

My heart began to pound. Janet has been in the prophetic dance ministry for decades and a dancer for decades before then. I wasn't sure how she'd react. As the song began, I was nervous, but as I worshipped and interpreted the lyrics prophetically, all of that faded away, and I enjoyed it. Afterward, she spoke words of life and encouragement over me. She told me that I wasn't just a ministry dancer or flagger but that I truly am a prophetic dancer. I cried tears of joy, as it felt like God was saying, "Do you see it now?"

I do. I see and understand more of what He is calling me to do. Janet said that every moment had purpose and that even my facial expressions shared the glory of the Lord.

I'm ready, Lord!

Today, I woke up sore from the over two and a half hours of dancing and flagging with Janet. We discussed technique and music choices. I didn't want it to end. I want to do it again right now!

I posted a few videos online of the different flags, and I can't stop watching them myself. I want more of this! It's the next best thing to writing for me. I feel so connected to God in the moment, listening to songs about Him, to Him, and about how He feels about us. It's personal. It's intimate.

I'm not sure what exactly is next, except that I will carve out time to practice and work on technique. I'll continue to seek opportunities for God to use me and this new gift He has affirmed in me. Of course, I'll continue to write. He's already mapped out the next, now *fifteen* ministry books (and another thirty titles on the list) and about eight business books. So it looks like writing and dancing are in my future, and I couldn't be more thrilled.

As we start my birthday week tomorrow, I can't help but reflect and laugh at how this started with the song "Something Has to Break" by Kierra Sheard.

I feel it in this room
Holy Spirit move
'Cause when you have Your way
Something has to break[4]

Those nineteen words sum up what has transpired over the past three months. My will, my ego, my plans all had to break. Y'all, there is beauty in brokenness. Move, and let your souls respond to the glory of God.

Chapter 20

Stay in the Hold
Saturday, February 11, 2023

So much has happened in the last two weeks. I officially turned fifty, spoke at an intimate event, and am scheduled to present four workshops next week at a women's retreat. Guess what's on the agenda? The Fuzzy Dice Formula! Yep, that's the official name of the exercise with the dice I mentioned earlier in the book. I'll be donning my fluffiest tutu as I present this workshop. Four hours of helping other women understand what is possible with God. I can't wait!

Sadly, I also received a skin cancer diagnosis this week, and we put our last family pet down. Our sweet Jack Russell, Maggie Grace. This will be the first book in which she isn't listed in my bio. She was my Snoopy—the most loyal dog this non-dog person has ever loved. I can't believe how much I miss her.

In the midst of uncertainty and grief, I'm choosing to turn toward all that is good in my life and enjoy the blessings. The skin cancer is treatable and at this point just a minor inconvenience with additional doctor's appointments and procedures. I won't get ahead of myself here, and I will choose to trust God. After all, He has many books still for me to write.

Remember in the last chapter, I shared how God mapped out fifteen ministry books on my to-be-written list? Well, how quickly that has changed. It's now nineteen! In total, I have five "Worth" series outlined. Each series has five pieces: a memoir, a Bible study, a journal, a process book, and a children's book. Yes, children's books!

My oldest grandson said he wanted to write a book with me the spring before his ninth birthday. I asked him what it would be about, and well, the rest as they say is history. Not published yet and still in the writing stages is my first fiction book. I'm over-the-moon excited to see how God is unfolding this and how it fits with each of the series in what I'm calling "The Worth Collection." Outside of *The Worth Collection*, I have at least two additional series He's shown me, along with two additional business series.

If, like my husband, you're wondering where this new prophetic dance ministry is taking me, allow me to let you in on what I know so far. It can be overwhelming when God calls us to new things. Over the past few weeks, I've found myself trying once again to figure it all out. But as God always does when we lean in, He spoke at another "Encounter" event earlier this week at my friend's church. It was an absolutely beautiful night of worship, and I danced freely as I poured my heart out to God, asking what to do with all of this He has so graciously given me. He didn't respond in that moment, but when I began to journal moments later, He whispered, "Stay in my embrace." I kept writing, "Stay in His hold."

At this most recent "Encounter," the speaker, Melissa Herring, brought a powerful message about altars. She described an altar as a place where we encounter God. In the Old Testament, they used to make altars at the places where they had experienced God. They would pile rocks and name the altar in remembrance of what God had done.

This brought two things to mind for me: first, the *Create Your Victory Channel* journal. That is exactly what this journal is—an altar. Each page is a rock, a remembrance of who God is and what He has done and will do again. Secondly, this book was on my mind. I've been saying for weeks now that I needed to get it to my editor. She's waiting on me. I'd like to sound all holy and say I was waiting on God to finish it, but the truth is, I was in my own head again.

Melissa said something to the effect of not letting the expectation of promise in our hearts become fantasy. She said instead to let God fulfill it. That is exactly why I documented my carpet meeting with God and the process of walking it out. I want to see God fulfill His promises in every area of my life, and it starts with my obedience.

As I close out this book, I'm pleading with you to be bold in your response to God's encounters. He has big things planned for you. His Word tells us so.

I know that I am to use my gifts of prophesying, writing, problem-solving, and dancing to bring glory to God. Currently, God is using my service strengths to help others understand their purpose and pursue their callings; for those called to write, I am to help them publish their books. I will stay in the hold and follow where He leads. If you need guidance or help walking out your purpose, or if you have a group of women you'd like me to pour into, let's chat. Whatever you do, don't close this book without committing to moving on His behalf.

There are two quotes (authors unknown) I came across while working on this project that I'd love to leave you with.

"The purpose of the human experience is to release heaven on earth."

I feel we do this by using our gifts to the glory of the Lord. Whatever your servant strengths are, use them! Allow the Holy Spirit to work and speak through you and heaven will be released on earth.

"Art is bringing into material existence that which only existed in the soul."

Let me guess: When you read this, if you consider yourself an artist, you leaned in and loved it. If you don't consider yourself an artist, you may have disregarded it. But I want you to go back and substitute your gift for the word *art*. Is your gift cooking? Encouraging? Dancing? Healing? Comforting? Teaching? They all fit. That's what happens when we are made in the image of our Creator.

In Chapter 17, I mentioned Shelley and concluding with her comment. I wish I could remember it exactly, but it confirmed the revelation I shared in Chapter 16 about learning who you are while responding to God. We don't have to clean ourselves up or figure ourselves out. We just need to follow the One who cleanses us and knows precisely what He created us for ... His glory. Want to know who you are? You are a vessel to reveal His glory! Go back to the quote above. When you boldly respond to encountering God, you are bringing into material existence that which only existed in the soul. Sincerely I ask, will you be a moved soul—so moved by the glory of God that you are willing to move on His behalf—*will you*?

Help Others

You can help others boldly respond to God by leaving a review for this book on Amazon or your other favorite online book retailer. I personally read and appreciate each review. Thank you for your support in my effort to glorify God through my writing.

ACKNOWLEDGMENTS

I acknowledge God and His crazy calling throughout this book, but I have to acknowledge Him again. I'm so thankful that He loves me and believes in me enough to not only call me to something so exhilarating but also to send His Son to die for me. I will worship You, O Lord, with all that I am.

Through weepy eyes, I want to thank Andrea Fehr for praying with me and over me. Thank you for being the kind of friend I hope that I am to others. Everyone needs an Andrea in their lives!

Thank you to my photography team at JME Studios in Tyler, Texas. Jamie Goode, you made me feel beautiful every step of the way and captured the joy of the Lord! I'm beyond thrilled about this cover shot, the back-cover headshot, and those I'll use on another book later this year! You *are* a moved soul, and I'm honored to have worked with you on this project. Thank you for your long nights of editing and for the kindness you continue to pour out. Thank you for introducing me to Meagan Brown.

Meagan, thank you for transforming me with your talent as a hair and makeup artist and for staying on set all day. My curls never looked so good! You went above and beyond. It's a day I will never forget.

To my friends and family at my January 7, 2023, birthday party—thank you for indulging me and for loving me. I pray you felt His presence.

To my hubs—what can I say? Thank you for praying with me daily. Thank you for loving me through all of the wild adventures and for creating so many for us. I pray my obedience in this calling will bless our family for years and generations to come.

About the Author

Brenda's had over forty jobs and has been working since she was twelve. She's never been fired and is not ashamed of her work history. Brenda always worked her way up, out, and on to the next adventure. Many see this as risky and call her fearless. She would tell you that fear was always a factor, she just chose faith instead.

After being told she was a nobody by a publisher, Brenda struggled with her identity as a writer. Not one to give up, she pursued her dream and released her first book, *Save the Butter Tubs!: Discover Your Worth in a Disposable World*, in 2018.

Brenda was immediately hired by her publishing agency after her book was released, and she went on to become the president of the company. An entrepreneur at heart, once again she left on top and now uses her experience to serve individuals and small businesses around the world as the CEO and co-founder of Joy of Pursuit. Brenda, the creator and coach of the Author Business Network, and her business partner, Amanda J. Painter, help writers go from overwhelmed, unsure, and distracted to confident, published, and building a business around their message. Additionally, they work with small business owners, guiding them through HR practices and publishing books to position themselves in the marketplace.

As a speaker, Brenda shares keynotes and workshops that transform audiences. Whether she is speaking about purpose, publishing, or small business, her deepest desire is to help you shine your light by operating in your grace-given gifts. She considers herself a moved soul—so moved by her encounters with God that she can't help but move. She wants the same for you—to encounter God in a way that you can't help but live a life worthy of your calling.

"Bebe" (as her grands call her) and her hubs (as she lovingly refers to him on social media), Darren, aka "Papa," are both military veterans. They enjoy hiking and chasing waterfalls across the United States and live in Texas with their beautifully blended and expanding family.

From Fear, Overthinking, and Shame to Freedom, Clarity, and Victory

Let Brenda guide you in
The Pursuit Process course.

BrendaHaire.com/Pursuit-Process-Course

Wow Your Audience with "The How"

From discovering your purpose to publishing a book, the Process Queen has you covered!

Make It Unique

Allow Brenda to usher in the Glory of God with a Prophetic Dance specifically for your event.

Save Your Date
BrendaHaire.com/Speaker

STAY CONNECTED

Brenda shares monthly resources and reminders to support you as you pursue God. Get yours at BrendaHaire.com.

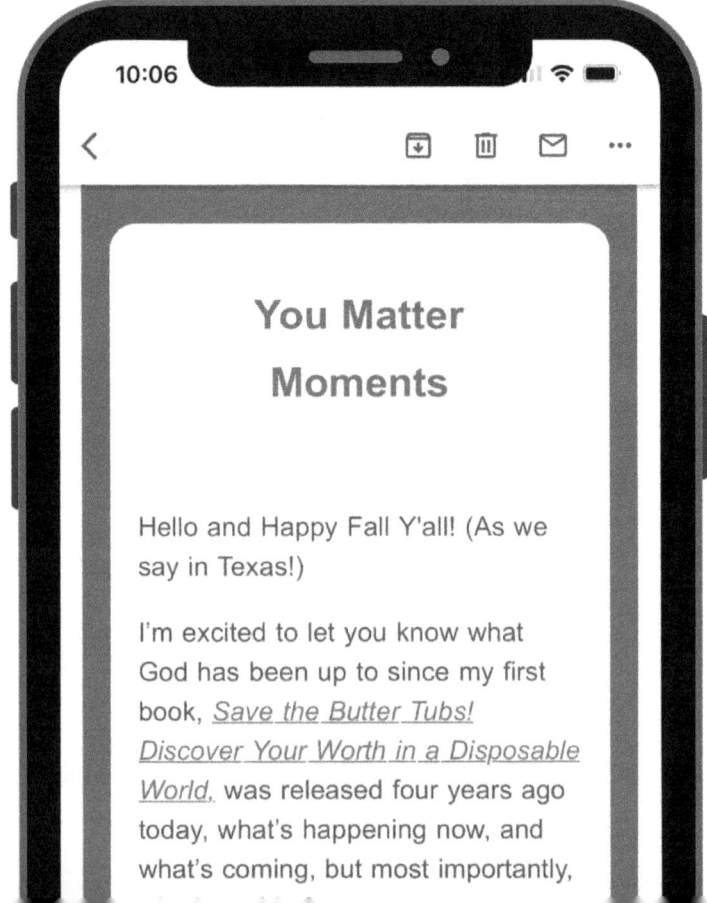

You Matter Moments

Hello and Happy Fall Y'all! (As we say in Texas!)

I'm excited to let you know what God has been up to since my first book, *Save the Butter Tubs! Discover Your Worth in a Disposable World,* was released four years ago today, what's happening now, and what's coming, but most importantly,

Have you ever thought about writing a book?

Work with Brenda!

In her membership, Brenda helps writers go from overwhelmed, unsure, and distracted to confident, published, and building a business around their message.

The Author Business NETWORK

TheJoyOfPursuit.com/Membership-Network

Buy in Bulk or in Sets

For Your Small Groups, as Gifts, or for Event Participants.

BrendaHaire.com/Shop

The Worth Collection

Saving

Pursuing

Knowing

Trusting

Following

Forgiving

Having

Receiving

Loving

BrendaHaire.com/Books

1. Written by Emmy Rose, Michaela Gentile, and Jessie Early. "Tend." Simple. Bethel Music Publishing (BMI) / Jessie Parker Early Music (BMI) / Capitol CMG Paragon (BMI), 2021.
2. Peters, Moriah. "Well Done." Provident Label Group LLC, a unit of Sony Music Entertainment, 2012.
3. Nichols, Morgan Harper. "Storyteller." Syntax Creative. 2017.
4. Sheard, Kierra; Fields, Mia; Smith, Jonathan; Sheard, J. Drew. "Something Has to Break." Upside Down Under (BMI), Be Essential Songs (BMI)/ Cashagamble Jet Music (BMI) (admin at Essential Music Publishing). 2020.

Testimonials

U nderstand, not everyone is called to be a prophetic dancer. I believe Brenda is anointed and appointed for this call. This is one of the many callings upon her life. She is allowing God to stretch her and use her in this new way. As I watched her dance before the Lord, her movements interpreted the song. This is what a prophetic dancer does. We speak with every movement. You could feel the presence of God upon her as she danced! I will joyfully continue to mentor her in this calling. My prayer is that she will usher in the presence of God when she moves through dance in such a way that the anointing will heal the sick, cast out demons, bring salvation to the lost and backslidden, heal the brokenhearted and do whatever else God desires through His willing vessel. Praise Jesus for her willingness to boldly respond to this calling! If you have the opportunity to witness her dancing or bring her to an event, you will be blessed.
—**Janet C.**

It was like the song came alive—spiritually drawn to the Holy Spirit! Brenda's interpretation of the song gave me goosebumps. I felt His presence. This is a wonderful way to express to others the way God moves in us. Wonderfully done! —**Angela M.**

I was in total awe when I heard the backstory of how Brenda learned to dance with the flags, which she described as an act of worship. It was a surprise to those of us in attendance, as Brenda explained the way God guided her, and with so little practice, it was the most graceful, amazing dance I have ever seen. I had seen others dance with flags in worship before, just not like this. It was like she was one with the flags, floating in front of us to a beautiful song. I was so touched by Brenda and her chosen song that I became emotional with gentle tears of euphoria as I felt and knew the Lord was in her heart like I have never known about anyone else before. *Beautiful*, *amazing*, and *graceful* seem like just words, as it was so much more—truly an act of worship. —**Jenifer H.**

I wish I could put into words what I experience each time I witness Brenda enter into true, deep worship through her dancing. The connection between Brenda and her Heavenly Father is literally palpable. It is so powerful that you are drawn into that intimately connected worship right beside her...it truly moves your soul. —**Kat W.**

www.ingramcontent.com/pod-product-compliance
Lightning Source LLC
Chambersburg PA
CBHW051526120626

46551CB00012B/1098